A Letter From The General

A play in Three Acts by

Maurice McLoughlin

Samuel French — London
New York - Toronto - Hollywood

Copyright © 1962 by Maurice McLoughlin
All Rights Reserved

A LETTER FROM THE GENERAL is fully protected under the copyright laws of the British Commonwealth, including Canada, the United States of America, and all other countries of the Copyright Union. All rights, including professional and amateur stage productions, recitation, lecturing, public reading, motion picture, radio broadcasting, television and the rights of translation into foreign languages are strictly reserved.

ISBN 978-0-573-01231-0

www.samuelfrench.co.uk

www.samuelfrench.com

For Amateur Production Enquiries

United Kingdom and World excluding North America

plays@samuelfrench.co.uk

020 7255 4302/01

Each title is subject to availability from Samuel French, depending upon country of performance.

CAUTION: Professional and amateur producers are hereby warned that *A LETTER FROM THE GENERAL* is subject to a licensing fee. Publication of this play does not imply availability for performance. Both amateurs and professionals considering a production are strongly advised to apply to the appropriate agent before starting rehearsals, advertising, or booking a theatre. A licensing fee must be paid whether the title is presented for charity or gain and whether or not admission is charged.

The Professional Rights in this play are controlled by Samuel French Ltd, 24-32 Stephenson Way, London NW1 2HD.

No one shall make any changes in this title for the purpose of production. No part of this book may be reproduced, stored in a retrieval system, or transmitted in any form, by any means, now known or yet to be invented, including mechanical, electronic, photocopying, recording, videotaping, or otherwise, without the prior written permission of the publisher. No one shall upload this title, or part of this title, to any social media websites.

The right of Maurice McLoughlin to be identified as author of this work has been asserted in accordance with Section 77 of the Copyright, Designs and Patents Act 1988.

A LETTER FROM THE GENERAL

Produced by The Mercat Theatre Trust at the Edinburgh Festival on the 19th August 1961, with the following cast of characters—

(in the order of their appearance)

SISTER HENRY	*Lennox Milne*
SISTER LUCY	*Helena Gloag*
SISTER BRIDGET	*Morag Forsyth*
REVEREND MOTHER	*Valerie Lush*
SISTER MAGDALEN	*Jean Taylor Smith*
ARTHUR STILTON, the British Consul	*John Young*
RUTH STILTON, his wife	*Irene Sunters*
CAPTAIN LEE	*Paul Kermack*
FATHER SCHILLER	*Martin Heller*

Directed by GERARD SLEVIN
Setting by JOHN RUSSELL

SYNOPSIS OF SCENES

The action of the Play passes in the Common Room of a Mission Station in an Eastern Country in the year 1950

ACT I

Afternoon

ACT II

SCENE 1 The evening of the same day
SCENE 2 The next morning

ACT III

The evening of the same day

COPYRIGHT INFORMATION

(See also page ii)

This play is fully protected under the Copyright Laws of the British Commonwealth of Nations, the United States of America and all countries of the Berne and Universal Copyright Conventions.

All rights including Stage, Motion Picture, Radio, Television, Public Reading, and Translation into Foreign Languages, are strictly reserved.

No part of this publication may lawfully be reproduced in ANY form or by any means—photocopying, typescript, recording (including video-recording), manuscript, electronic, mechanical, or otherwise—or be transmitted or stored in a retrieval system, without prior permission.

Licences for amateur performances are issued subject to the understanding that it shall be made clear in all advertising matter that the audience will witness an amateur performance; that the names of the authors of the plays shall be included on all programmes; and that the integrity of the authors' work will be preserved.

The Royalty Fee is subject to contract and subject to variation at the sole discretion of Samuel French Ltd.

In Theatres or Halls seating Six Hundred or more the fee will be subject to negotiation.

In Territories Overseas the fee quoted above may not apply. A fee will be quoted on application to our local authorized agent, or if there is no such agent, on application to Samuel French Ltd, London.

VIDEO RECORDING OF AMATEUR PRODUCTIONS

Please note that the copyright laws governing the video-recording are extremely complex and that it should not be assumed that any play may be video-recorded for whatever purpose without first obtaining the permission of the appropriate agents. The fact that a play is published by Samuel French Ltd does not indicate that video rights are available or that Samuel French Ltd controls such rights.

A LETTER FROM THE GENERAL

ACT I

SCENE—*The Common Room of a Mission Station in an Eastern Country in the year 1950. Afternoon.*

The room is painted white and the walls are bare of decoration except for a crucifix hanging on the wall down R. *There is a latticed door back* C *with windows* R *and* L *of it, leading to a verandah. In the distance stretches a plain in a haze of heat. Mostly the door is closed and the glare of the sun makes rigid bars of light which pierce the lattices and window blinds. Another door, down* L, *leads to other parts of the Mission. The room is simply furnished. A large table, used as a desk, stands at an angle* RC, *with upright chairs behind and* L *of it. A small desk is set against the wall* R, *underneath the crucifix. A large cupboard, filled with miscellaneous household articles stands against the wall* L, *above the door. There are shelves, filled with books, up* R, *up* L *and under the window* L *of the door up* C. *An upright chair is down* L *and there is a light, bamboo-type armchair down* RC. *At night, the room is lit by oil lamps, one on the desk* R *and one hanging from a wall-bracket above the door* L.

When the CURTAIN *rises,* SISTER HENRY, *a nun, is standing at the table* RC *with a pile of books beside her, which she is listing. She wears a white habit and is a woman of forty with sharp features and a thin, tight-lipped mouth. She crosses to the shelves up* L, *takes out some books and brings them to the table.* SISTER LUCY, *a plump, plain nun, appears outside the open window up* LC. *She is red-faced and perspires from working in the sun.*

LUCY (*calling through the window*) Have you seen the pliers anywhere, Sister Henry?
HENRY. No.
LUCY. I've searched all over the Mission. I'd say one of the Ling family has taken them. (*She comes in by the door up* C) It's terrible thieves they are. (*She moves to the cupboard up* L) You didn't see them in that cupboard?
HENRY. I haven't looked in the cupboard.
LUCY. You'd never believe the rubbish that's thrown in this cupboard. (*She opens the cupboard door and a stream of miscellaneous rubbish falls to the floor*) There now, didn't I tell you? I'm not tidying that lot. (*She makes a dive into the pile*) Well, if it isn't the china salt cellar we were scouring the Mission for. Now what would that be doing in there?
HENRY. I couldn't say at all.
LUCY. It's certain you are that you haven't set eyes on the

pliers? Before I sort out this jumble? Do you know what they're like, Sister Henry?

HENRY (*turning; coldly*) Sister Lucy, I'm not given to doing odd jobs about the Mission but I can recognize a pair of pliers when I set eyes on them. Why is there all this agitation for the pliers?

LUCY. The wire in the chicken compound is in shreds. If it's not repaired you'll have the soldiers eating every chicken we've got. Ling Hu is after telling me there's another lot of them at the village.

HENRY. You'll find the soldiers will have the chickens eventually.

LUCY. You mean we shall have to go? Sure I wouldn't say that. We've not had the word to leave.

HENRY. Perhaps not. But it's obvious if we stay we shall be cut off from the villagers and the children. They came and took the orphans from us, didn't they? (*She turns to the bookshelves up* R)

LUCY. Reverend Mother says it has all happened before. It might well come to nothing.

HENRY (*turning; with feeling*) And meanwhile we stay here in splendid isolation, providing religious solace to thirty-three chickens.

LUCY. Thirty-two. There was another taken in the night. Did Sister Magdalen tell you she'd written to the General? He's the new Governor of the Province.

HENRY. Do you seriously think that Sister Magdalen's letter to General Mei Cheng will do anything but remind him of our existence and bring a firing squad to visit us?

LUCY. Sister Magdalen says he was a fine boy. He knew his Catechism better than she did herself. Sure he's her godson. Can you think of it—godmother to a General.

HENRY. A communist General who'd put a bullet through you as soon as he'd look at you.

LUCY. That we can't say. He may well be the beginning of better things for us.

HENRY. Have sense, Sister Lucy. You know as well as I do myself that the next thing we shall have is an order to leave the country—if we're fortunate. For myself I'd be more inclined to expect a troop of soldiers to arrest us. I can't think why Reverend Mother doesn't arrange with the British Consul for us to leave immediately, while we have opportunity. (*She picks up some books from the desk, crosses and puts them in the shelves up* L)

LUCY (*kneeling at the cupboard*) There's no use thinking about it. We'll have to wait and see.

HENRY. I didn't join the Order to be a sort of Sanctified Micawber.

LUCY. You've never liked it here, Sister Henry.

HENRY (*crossing to the table*) I've no love for any country where I have to sit idle. At least if we go suddenly the schoolbooks will be in order. I'm listing them now,

LUCY (*rising*) I wish I could find the pliers. I think I'll be asking St Anthony to find them for me.

(HENRY *sits above the table*)

He's a wonderful saint, with eyes in the back of his head. (*She suddenly pulls the pliers from the rubbish*) Look, Sister Henry—it's them—the pliers. His name had hardly left my lips and the things were in my hand. He's a wonderful man—St Anthony.

HENRY (*dryly*) I should hurry away and repair the chicken wire or you'll have him chasing all over the Province after your chickens.

LUCY (*crossing to* L *of Henry; shocked*) Sister Henry, you shouldn't speak in that way of a Saint of God. St Anthony is . . .

HENRY (*cutting in*) I apologize, Sister Lucy.

(SISTER BRIDGET *appears outside the window up* LC. *She is a young and very beautiful nun in her early twenties. She is garrulous and full of enthusiasm and wild exaggeration*)

BRIDGET (*speaking through the window*) I can't find the pliers, Sister Lucy. I should think the last fellah we had working round the place has taken them, or maybe one of the Ling family. They're terrible thieves. (*She comes in by the door up* C *and sees the pliers in Lucy's hand*) Ah, sure you've found them. Where were they?

LUCY. I turned out the cupboard and there they were. Shove it in again, will you, Bridget? (*She moves to the door up* C) If I don't mend the wire we'll have the chickens in Hong Kong. (*She goes on to the verandah*)

BRIDGET (*moving to the cupboard*) I hope that white cockerel gets away. He has a mean way with him.

(LUCY *stops outside the window up* LC)

Only this morning he pecked at the small hen with the white underside. (*A thought*) Why wouldn't we eat him, Sister Lucy? I must search in my Missal and find a Saint's day that calls for a chicken.

LUCY (*through the window*) 'Tis Reverend Mother's Feast Day next month. That would call for a chicken, maybe.

HENRY. If we are here next month.

BRIDGET (*eagerly*) Have we heard anything? Do we have to go?

LUCY. Of course not. Don't you think Reverend Mother would have told us?

BRIDGET. And Magdalen is after writing to the General. I'd like to see a General. My father was a great friend of Michael Collins. He had a big picture of him lying in state. It hung in the kitchen.

LUCY. He was a fine man was Michael Collins.

HENRY. He compromised and paid the penalty for compromising.

BRIDGET (*with fire*) My father says he was murdered. (*She crosses to* L *of Henry*) He says he was the finest man you'd ever meet.

HENRY. I wasn't discussing the man's character—only his lack of political foresight.

LUCY. Oh, let's not talk politics. They're not for us. Put that junk in the cupboard, Bridget. I'll attend to the wire. We'll not have a chicken left—although I've put a board before the hole.

(LUCY *exits* L *on the verandah.*

BRIDGET *crosses to the cupboard, pushes the rubbish in and closes the door.*

HENRY *rises and crosses to the shelves up* LC)

BRIDGET. Well, the cupboard is shut. Although if anyone opens the door there'll be an avalanche. (*She turns to Henry*) You're anxious to go from here, aren't you, Sister Henry?

HENRY. Of course I am.

BRIDGET. Do you think it's the truth that they're shooting nuns and priests in some of the provinces?

HENRY (*crossing to the table*) I see no reason why it shouldn't be. I've no particular desire to stay here and find out. (*She sits at the table*)

BRIDGET (*moving down* LC) We'd be martyrs, then. Although I'm wondering if it counts if you get shot out of hand like that. I mean, you'd have no choice at all. And somehow I always think of martyrs having a white gown and fair hair, holding a flower with their faces all lit up. It's like as not they'd line up the lot of us against the chicken run and kill us with machine guns. It doesn't seem right—not machine guns.

HENRY. Maybe the General having had a good Christian education will give us a white gown and flowers.

BRIDGET. Sister Magdalen says he was the nicest boy she ever taught. (*She crosses to* L *of Henry*) Did she ever tell you he was her godson?

HENRY. She told me thirty times and everyone else has told me eighty times. I find it a great consolation.

BRIDGET (*crossing above Henry to* R *of the desk*) Well, I shall be sorry to go even if you aren't. I like these people and the children. I don't think Reverend Mother will go without a fight. Where is she? I've hardly seen her all day. (*She picks up a book and glances through it*)

HENRY. I don't know. She has plenty of work to keep her in her room. This is the only other habitable room and it's as conducive to work as O'Connell Street.

BRIDGET. Am I disturbing you? What are you doing?

HENRY. I'm trying to make an inventory of school books and equipment.

BRIDGET. I must away and attend to the Ling family. I wish they'd keep their hut a little cleaner. One thing—no-one has forbidden them to come to the Mission. And it's as well for they attend the crops well enough. And Ling Hu is a wonderful lad for catching fish.

(*The* REVEREND MOTHER *enters* L *and crosses to* C. *She is a short, strong woman of sixty. Her face is yellow from years in the tropics. She has a soft, authoritative voice and light blue eyes with a magnetic quality about them.* HENRY *is about to rise*)

REV. MOTHER. Don't bother to rise, Sister Henry.

BRIDGET (*crossing to the Reverend Mother*) Oh, Reverend Mother, there's a great hole in the chicken compound. Sister Lucy is mending it now for fear the chickens would be all over the province.

REV. MOTHER. Good. We can't afford to lose any. Were there many eggs today?

BRIDGET. Twenty-two. I'm thinking Ling Hu is after stealing some of them and that's how the hole came in the wire.

REV. MOTHER. That's likely enough, but he knows we don't begrudge him a few eggs. And it gives him such pleasure to take them subversively. The family have a great deal to put up with.

(HENRY *rises and crosses to the shelves up* L)

BRIDGET. I've been trying to convert them, Reverend Mother, but the old man quotes Confucius at me till I'm dizzy. Do you know, I think he's trying to convert *me*.

REV. MOTHER (*crossing to* RC) Now don't let him do that, Bridget. We can ill afford any deviationists. Have you attended them this morning?

BRIDGET. I was just away when you came in. (*She moves to the door up* C *and turns*) Is there any news, Reverend Mother? I mean —about us going?

REV. MOTHER. No, Sister Bridget. I'll surely tell you when I have definite news.

BRIDGET. No answer from the General to Sister Magdalen's letter?

REV. MOTHER. No, child. But then it's quite possible that he never received the letters.

BRIDGET (*moving* C) He'd surely answer a letter from his godmother. Yes, I'd say he never had the letter at all. She should surely write again.

(*The* REVEREND MOTHER *looks at Bridget*)

(*She hurries to the door up* C) When I've tended the Lings I'll give Sister Magdalen a hand with the evening meal. She looks tired.

(BRIDGET, *humming to herself, exits up* C)

REV. MOTHER (*turning to Henry*) A fine girl she is, so contented in herself and her work. What are you at, Sister Henry?

HENRY (*moving* LC) I'm listing the school books and equipment.
REV. MOTHER. That's as well. In case we have to close the Mission.
HENRY. Reverend Mother, do we have to sit here until we're told to go? Isn't it possible to ask the Consul to arrange for us to close the Mission and be on the next boat down the river?
REV. MOTHER. For the moment I think we have a duty to stay here.
HENRY. But why? What are we doing here? The school is closed. Our children snatched from us and the villagers forbidden to come near us. It seems so pointless.
REV. MOTHER. You must have patience, Sister Henry. Our staying here at the moment is far from pointless. I have an excellent reason for doing so.
HENRY. Have you heard from Reverend Mother Provincial?
REV. MOTHER. Not for months.
HENRY. And what of Father Schiller? He's not been near us for three months. Is it reasonable for us to stay here caring for thirty-three chickens and without a priest to visit us? I see no sense in it.
REV. MOTHER. Conditions may not always be as they are now. Revolutions come and go but the Church of God is indestructible. You must accept my word that I know what I am doing is right.
HENRY (*moving down* L) I do, Reverend Mother. I would just like to see why it is right. (*Bitterly*) Five nuns to care for a few chickens and a family of diseased Bhuddists.
REV. MOTHER (*sharply*) I prefer you not to speak that way, Sister Henry. You must learn to guard your tongue.
HENRY (*about to flare up*) I can say . . . (*She stops*) I apologize, Reverend Mother.
REV. MOTHER. Believe me now, I have every sympathy for you. (*She crosses to Henry*) Have patience. You'll surely have great opportunities to teach again. Meantime—pray for patience. Now, if you'll leave your inventory for a minute I'd like to see a list of the children that were taken from us. Can you get the names from the registers?
HENRY. Yes, Reverend Mother. I'll do so at once.

(HENRY *exits up* C. *The* REVEREND MOTHER *moves to the table and sits at it.*
SISTER MAGDALEN *enters* L. *She is a very old nun and wears large spectacles which give her an owlish appearance. Her voice is soft and gentle. She holds a piece of paper*)

MAGDALEN (*crossing to* L *of the table*) It's here you are, Reverend Mother. I've searched the Mission for you.
REV. MOTHER. I've been in my room, Sister Magdalen. Sit down, won't you?
MAGDALEN (*ignoring the invitation to sit*) I'd like you to see this.

Act I A LETTER FROM THE GENERAL 7

'Tis what I'm after writing to Peter. (*She hands the letter to the Reverend Mother*)

REV. MOTHER. Thank you. (*She reads the letter*)

(LUCY *enters up* C, *carrying the pliers*)

LUCY (*moving down* C) Them chickens'll not get out of there so fast now. Reverend Mother, do you think we might have that white cockerel for eating on your feast day? (*She realizes she is interrupting*) Oh, I beg your pardon.

MAGDALEN. I'm after writing to Peter, again. Would you read out the letter, Reverend Mother? I'd like Sister Lucy to hear what I've written. (*She sits* L *of the desk*)

REV. MOTHER (*reading slowly*) "Dear Peter . . ."

MAGDALEN (*interrupting*) Do you see I call him "Peter" for he was baptized "Peter". Sure he's a General now, but 'tis only right for his godmother to call him by his Christian name. Wouldn't you say that?

REV. MOTHER. Yes, indeed. "Dear Peter. As I haven't heard from you I feel sure that you have not received my letters. We at the Mission here have not had a letter for three months. Did you know that our Mission has been cut off from the village and all our dear little children have been taken from us? We have been very happy here and I am sure that if the authorities knew the good work we have done they would let us open the Mission once more. It is twenty years now since we last met and I was delighted to hear that the Japanese had released you, and that later you were made a General of the army. I remember still the first day you came to our Mission, a bright little boy and it was my first year in your country. I feel now as if it were my country, too."

MAGDALEN. Thirty years this month, Reverend Mother.

REV. MOTHER (*reading*) "Our present Mission is not unlike the one in the North where you spent so many happy years. I do wish you could come here and meet our Reverend Mother. She has done wonderful work for your people." (*She pauses*)

MAGDALEN. Indeed you have, Reverend Mother.

REV. MOTHER (*reading*) "I am sure that if you came you would be able to tell your Government how mistaken they are to close our Mission. You must try for a visit here—it would delight me to show you around. Fondest love. Your Mother in Jesus Christ, Magdalen O'Hara."

(*There is a moment's pause as the futility of the letter sinks into the* REVEREND MOTHER'S *consciousness*)

MAGDALEN (*eagerly*) Do you think it's a good letter, Reverend Mother?

REV. MOTHER (*with control*) An excellent letter, Sister Magdalen. I'm sure it will please him—if he gets it. (*She hands the letter to Magdalen*)

MAGDALEN (*rising and crossing to the door* L) I had thought that we might send it to the Officer at the village.
    REV. MOTHER. And why not? It's worth a try.
    MAGDALEN. And when you have a minute I'd like for you to look at the kitchen stove. I'm having great trouble with it and you have a way with the thing.
    REV. MOTHER (*rising and crossing to the door* L) I'll come right away.

  (MAGDALEN *holds the door open*)

(*To Lucy*) Tell Sister Bridget not to bother in the kitchen. I can help Sister Magdalen this afternoon. I want extra food, too. We must keep our strength up.
    LUCY. Talking of food—what about the white cockerel? Would we kill it for your feast day?
    REV. MOTHER. No, we shall have it tomorrow.
    LUCY. Sure Sister Bridget will be delighted. She has a great hatred for the white cockerel.
    REV. MOTHER. Come, Magdalen, let's see this terror of a stove.

  (*The* REVEREND MOTHER *and* MAGDALEN *exit* L. LUCY *goes to the cupboard to put the pliers away, opens the door and the jumble shoots out on to the floor. She is about to say something explosive then stops, makes a sign of the cross, kneels and starts to replace the jumble in the cupboard.*
    BRIDGET *enters excitedly up* C)

LUCY. I like fine the way you've put this rubbish in the cupboard.
    BRIDGET (*breathlessly*) Never mind that old stuff. There's a car coming down the driveway—a man and a woman—white people.
    LUCY. Didn't you wait to see who it was?

  (*The sound of a car arriving and stopping is heard off*)

BRIDGET. I thought I'd better be telling Reverend Mother.
    LUCY. Sure it'll be the Consul. He's the only man likely to come here. (*She rises*) I'll tell Reverend Mother. You'd better ask them in instead of standing there panting.
    BRIDGET. Let me tell Reverend Mother. I don't know their names.
    LUCY. Oh, sure 'tis "Bilton"—"Mr Bilton", I'm certain—or would it be "Hilton"? I disremember. Just tell them to wait a minute.

  (LUCY *rushes out* L)

BRIDGET. Sister Lucy! (*She turns towards the door up* C, *stops, looks at her dusty habit, turns and brushes it with her hand*)

  (ARTHUR STILTON, *the British Consul, and his wife* RUTH *enter* L *on the verandah. Stilton is aged about forty-five, slightly worn and* tired looking. *Ruth is in her late thirties, attractive with a dissatisfied air. She is as tall as her husband.* STILTON *looks in at the door up* C)

STILTON (*calling*) Anyone here?
BRIDGET (*turning; startled*) Oh, come in.

(STILTON *and* RUTH *come into the room.* RUTH *scrutinizes the room as if it were a personal affront*)

Won't you sit down, Mr Hilton?
STILTON. Thank you, Sister. My name is "Stilton".
BRIDGET (*losing all her poise*) "Stilton"! Now would you think anyone could forget a name like that? Why, you've only got to think of che— (*She stops*) I'll tell Reverend Mother you're here, sir.

(BRIDGET, *embarrassed, rushes out* L)

STILTON. Well, I'm damned!
RUTH (*moving to* L *of the table*) Is this where I'm expected to stay, Arthur? (*She carefully scrutinizes the armchair down* RC, *sits, takes a compact from her handbag and attends to her make-up*)
STILTON (*moving down* C) My dear Ruth, where else can you stay? It will only be for a couple of nights at the most. My God! I'll be glad to leave this country.
RUTH. You won't find me weeping at the thought. Why couldn't we go when the others left?
STILTON. Because it's my job to stay put until I get orders to leave.
RUTH. And I suppose it is my job to stay put with you.
STILTON. I think so. Why didn't you go last month if you were so anxious to leave?
RUTH. On that stinking train? No, thank you.
STILTON. You didn't expect me to let you go with McGregor in his car, did you? There's been quite enough between you and McGregor without any encouragement from me.
RUTH. He didn't ask me to go.
STILTON. He was waiting for me to suggest it and I didn't. I told him you would be leaving with me on the boat. (*He takes a flask from his pocket and drinks*)
RUTH (*watching him closely*) You'll make an excellent impression on the Reverend Mother reeking of spirits.
STILTON. I've already met her. She's surprisingly tolerant of human failings. You could tell her of McGregor—and Hastings.

(RUTH *gives Stilton a vicious look but says nothing*)

(*He takes another swig*) Yes. You'll find the Reverend Mother an intriguing combination of wisdom and innocence. So is Sister Magdalen, with more emphasis on the innocence. *She's* been here God knows how many years. General Mei Cheng was a prize pupil in her Mission School—so rumour has it.

RUTH. She must have been highly competent if her converts turn into Communist Generals. It's a wonder the Government want to close the place.

STILTON. You know the line—"Opium of the people". (*He wanders to the open door up* C, *leans against the door-post and looks off* L) Thank heaven they're going to be allowed to leave unharmed. Damned awkward when they shoot these missionaries out of hand.

RUTH (*sarcastically*) Very trying for the Consul. Reports to make and so on.

STILTON. You needn't be so damned sarcastic. It *is* awkward. "Why didn't you do something about it?" they ask. What the hell can the Consul do?

RUTH. Make a report.

STILTON. Thank God this is the last Mission in the Province. The sooner they're out safely the better.

RUTH. Didn't Mei Cheng arrest that German priest a couple of days ago?

STILTON. Father Schiller? Yes, but he's not my pigeon.

RUTH. Don't worry. I didn't intend to lose any sleep over him.

(*The* REVEREND MOTHER *enters* L. RUTH *rises and puts her handbag on the desk* R)

REV. MOTHER (*moving* LC *and extending her hand*) I'm pleased to see you, Mr Stilton.

STILTON (*moving to* R *of the Reverend Mother and shaking hands*) How do you do, Reverend Mother? This is my wife.

REV. MOTHER. Won't you sit down—both of you. (*She moves the chair* L *to* LC *and sits*)

(RUTH *resumes her seat.* STILTON *sits* L *of the table*)

Now, I don't suppose for a second this is a social call.

STILTON. Not exactly. The fact is, I've got some rather bad news for you.

REV. MOTHER. Yes?

STILTON. I'm afraid it's come to the point where you must close the Mission and leave. I've made arrangements to go by the river boat myself. It leaves in three days—and for your Community to come with me.

REV. MOTHER (*thoughtfully*) You have?

STILTON. Yes. I'm very sorry—but there it is. To be quite honest, I can't see any useful purpose in your staying here. I've made orders to close the Consulate so it is my duty to advise you to quit.

REV. MOTHER. And supposing I don't want to quit?

STILTON. What any of us wants doesn't arise. It's a question of being sensible. You may be sure the Foreign Office don't close the Consulate without good reason. You know the policy of this Government towards foreigners.

Act I   A LETTER FROM THE GENERAL

REV. MOTHER. Don't forget that I have to obey orders, Mr Stilton. I've had no instructions from my Mother General.

STILTON. I don't suppose your superiors have been in touch with you for the last three months, have they?

REV. MOTHER. They have not.

STILTON. Then how can they understand the situation here? (*He rises and moves to* R *of the Reverend Mother*) I'm on the spot at the Provincial capital. I can tell you that if you wait for instructions from outside you'll wait for ever.

REV. MOTHER. This sort of thing has occurred before. It'll pass.

STILTON (*firmly*) The Consulate has never been closed before. You can take it from me, the Revolution is over and the Government firmly in the saddle. There will be no change for a year or so—by then your Community will be wiped out.

REV. MOTHER. Wiped out?

STILTON (*pressing his point home*) Yes. Shot dead—after being tortured. It's happened in the North. (*Suddenly*) Didn't you wonder why you hadn't seen Father Schiller for weeks?

REV. MOTHER. What do you know about Father Schiller?

STILTON. Very little except that he was arrested a few days ago. He may be dead by now.

(*The* REVEREND MOTHER *rises and moves up* C)

(*More gently*) I'm sorry to break the news so harshly, Reverend Mother, but I'm trying to show there's no time to lose.

REV. MOTHER (*turning to face Stilton*) Do you know why Father Schiller was arrested?

STILTON. He was Father Schiller, a priest and a foreigner. The present policy is to make the arrest and think of the reason afterwards.

REV. MOTHER. You made no enquiries?

STILTON. Of course not. He's nothing to do with me. Father Schiller is a German.

RUTH. If they didn't shoot him at once he'll be deported.

REV. MOTHER (*crossing to* L *of Ruth*) Did you know Father Schiller, Mrs Stilton?

RUTH (*sharply*) No.

REV. MOTHER. He's given his life for this country. It seems a poor reward to be arrested on a trumped-up charge as though he were a criminal. He's done nothing but good for the people here. Don't you see that, Mr Stilton?

STILTON. I'm afraid my views wouldn't count for very much even if I made a protest. My duty at the moment is to see that you and your Community are conducted to safety without any trouble. So I should advise you to be ready when the boat arrives at the village.

REV. MOTHER. Of course I'm grateful to you for coming here.

STILTON. It is my duty. You know that. I want to ask you a

favour. I have to go to a village up the river to warn an English writer. He must be made aware of the situation, not that I think he will take much notice of me—but it is my job. I'd like you to let Mrs Stilton stay here until I return.

Rev. Mother. We shall be delighted for her to stay.

Stilton. I ought to be back by tomorrow but it's not the sort of country to take her under present conditions.

Rev. Mother. We'll do our best to make her comfortable and that isn't easy at present. We've lost our native helpers, but there's plenty of accommodation. I hope it doesn't prove too primitive for Mrs Stilton.

Stilton. You won't mind for a couple of days, will you, Ruth?

Ruth. Anything would be preferable to a long drive over those roads, but if the Reverend Mother would be put out at all . . .

Rev. Mother. We can manage well enough. (*She crosses to the chair* LC *and returns it to its original place*) I'll have Sister Lucy prepare a room for you.

Ruth. You said you'd lost your native helpers, but didn't I see some of them in a hut just off the drive-in?

Rev. Mother. They're the Ling family. The authorities don't want the likes of them. They're glad to leave them here.

(Henry *enters up* C)

Henry (*seeing the visitors*) I apologize, Reverend Mother. I didn't know there were visitors.

Rev. Mother. Come in, Sister Henry. This is Mr Stilton, the Consul, and his wife. Mrs Stilton is going to stay with us for a day or two. Perhaps you'd entertain them while I search out Sister Lucy. She'll prepare a room.

Ruth. Please don't go to any great trouble.

Rev. Mother. It's no trouble at all. (*To Stilton*) Sister Henry taught the older children at our school.

(*The* Reverend Mother *exits down* L)

Henry. What news have you for us, Mr Stilton?

Stilton. Bad, I'm afraid, Sister. I've just told the Reverend Mother that I want her to be gone in a couple of days.

Henry. I'd say it was the obvious thing to do.

Ruth (*interested*) You don't share the Reverend Mother's reluctance to leave?

Henry. I've no desire to leave my work. But at the moment we aren't doing any. I'd be surprised if they'd let us open the Mission again. Would you say it was possible, Mr Stilton?

Stilton. I'd say it was most unlikely and I think your attitude is most sensible, Sister Henry. Perhaps you can persuade the Reverend Mother to take the same view. I'm leaving myself and the Consulate is being closed. That should give you an idea of what we expect.

HENRY. Reverend Mother already knows my views, but if she really decides to stay, then I can do nothing but obey her.

RUTH. Now why? I can't understand. You're a free agent, aren't you? (*She smiles*) If she told you to jump off a cliff, would you do it?

HENRY. That's a contingency that isn't likely to arise.

RUTH. I think I'd sooner jump off a cliff than be in your position.

HENRY. But surely if you say we must go, there's no option, Mr Stilton.

STILTON (*crossing to the table*) I can't make you leave, Sister. It's my duty as Consul to make you aware of the situation, and advise you. I've even made arrangements for you to go.

HENRY. And Reverend Mother still says we stay here?

RUTH. She certainly doesn't jump at the idea of going. (*She rises, moves to the desk* R *and picks up her handbag*) By the way, they've put your Father Schiller in prison.

HENRY. They've arrested him? Why? (*She moves down* L *and faces front. Bitterly*) There's no need to ask why. I suppose in due course he'll sign a confession to heaven knows what devilry, and be shot.

STILTON. That seems to be the procedure in the North and you know how they get the signatures.

(*There is a silence*)

I'll collect your cases, Ruth, from the car. (*He moves to the door up* C) I'm sorry I have such bad news, Sister Henry. If you make the Reverend Mother see reason you'll be doing us all a favour.

(STILTON *exits up* C. RUTH *takes a cigarette case and matches from her handbag*)

RUTH. You don't mind if I smoke?

HENRY. Not at all.

(RUTH *lights a cigarette for herself*)

RUTH. You won't have one?

(HENRY *shakes her head*)

Not allowed to, I suppose? You'll have to get used to me. I don't mix with nuns a lot. In fact I'd never spoken to one until a month ago. (*She pauses*) What are you thinking about?

HENRY (*turning to face Ruth*) When did they arrest Father Schiller?

RUTH. A couple of weeks ago, I think.

HENRY. Your husband couldn't do *anything*?

RUTH. It was hardly his job. Schiller was a German.

HENRY. You don't sound terribly concerned about Father Schiller.

RUTH. I'm not. The only good Germans are dead ones.

HENRY (*acidly*) Isn't that a little out of date?

RUTH. If it's the truth it's never out of date. I don't expect you to share my views but don't try to correct them.
HENRY. I hadn't that intention.
RUTH. That's fine. As long as we understand one another. (*She sits in the armchair*) They tell me that one of your alumni is governing the Province, Mei Cheng.
HENRY. He was one of Sister Magdalen's pupils many years ago. Do you know the General?
RUTH. I met him when he came to see us about closing the Consulate.
HENRY. Did he force you to close it?
RUTH. No, that was orders from the Foreign Office. Mei Cheng said it was all the same to him whether we closed it or not. For my part he can have his stinking country.
HENRY. You don't like it here, Mrs Stilton?
RUTH. Do you?
HENRY. I like my work wherever it is.
RUTH. But you'd enjoy it a damned sight better if it weren't there?
HENRY (*moving to the window up* LC) I didn't say so. (*She gazes out of the window*)
RUTH. You people are beyond me. You allow yourself to be ordered about by whoever they like to put in charge of you. Even if they have the most hare-brained schemes.
HENRY. You'd be surprised how few hare-brained schemes our Superiors have.
RUTH. Well, attempting to stay here under the circumstances doesn't strike me as terribly bright. Still, that's your affair. Sixty Reverend Mothers wouldn't keep me off that boat in a couple of days.

(STILTON *enters up* C *carrying three suitcases which he places on the ground* LC)

STILTON. I'll leave most of my things here, Ruth. They can pick the trunks up at the village.
RUTH (*rising and moving below the table; crossly*) Are you leaving the trunks at that barracks?
STILTON. Yes.
RUTH. They'll probably all be stolen when you come back.
STILTON. I don't think so. The Commanding Officer seemed quite civil.
RUTH. That's their stock-in-trade here—civility. They could hang you up by your feet and look civil about it.
STILTON. We'll have to chance it.

(*The* REVEREND MOTHER *and* LUCY *enter* L)

REV. MOTHER. Ah, the bags. Sister Lucy would have helped you with them.
STILTON. I'm leaving now, if you don't mind, Reverend Mother. I want to get to this chap by tomorrow morning.

Rev. Mother. You'll be driving through the night?
Stilton. Yes, but I'll be all right. I've got my official permit for the journey. Think again, Reverend Mother. I hope you'll have decided to leave and be ready to go when I return. (*He crosses to Ruth*) Good-bye, Ruth.

(Stilton *gives Ruth a formal kiss, then exits up* c. *The* Reverend Mother *follows him as far as the door, then turns and moves down* c)

Rev. Mother. Sister Lucy will take you to your room, Mrs Stilton.

(*The sound is heard of a car starting up and driving away.* Lucy *picks up two of the cases and moves to the door* L)

We usually have a meal after Office.
Ruth. Office?
Rev. Mother. We have our prayers—our Office—at six-thirty, and a meal at seven. Unless you care for a meal now?
Ruth. No. Seven will do. You don't mind if I skip the prayers?
Rev. Mother. Do what you like, Mrs Stilton. Sister will show you the refectory—the dining-room. Come here if you want to read or sit quietly. It is the only room with any comfortable chairs just now. Use it as you will.
Ruth (*crossing to the door* L) Thank you very much.
Rev. Mother. I've given you the room Father Schiller used to have when he came here.
Ruth. Oh, yes. Well, I'll try not to be any trouble.
Rev. Mother. We shall make allowances for you, Mrs Stilton.

(Ruth *gives the Reverend Mother a sharp look, but her face remains guileless.*
Lucy *exits with two cases* L.
Ruth *picks up the remaining case and follows* Lucy *off*)

(*She moves to the table*) I'd say Mrs Stilton was an unhappy woman.
Henry (*gazing out of the window*) She has no unhappiness about leaving here. (*She turns*) So Father Schiller has been arrested? (*She moves to the door* L *and closes it*)
Rev. Mother (*sitting above the table*) Yes.
Henry. That means we shall be next—unless we leave with the Consul.
Rev. Mother. Only God knows that.
Henry. I know it. Are we going to wait here, Reverend Mother? Are we going to wait here to be murdered?
Rev. Mother. You sound very melodramatic, Sister Henry.
Henry. Being murdered is melodramatic, or would you call it an anticlimax? (*She moves to* L *of the table*) Reverend Mother, I have no wish to die. It's not fear in me, don't think that, but I've years of work in me yet. I don't want to be taken out and shot by the chicken run—not when a boat is waiting to take me to safety and

the chance to start my work over again. (*Earnestly*) Won't you see, it's different for yourself and Sister Magdalen. Your work is nearly done. But if I stay here and die, half my life will be gone to waste. I want to do what you've done yourself—leave something behind me.

Rev. Mother (*quietly*) And what shall I be leaving behind me, Sister Henry? (*She looks sadly around the room*)

Henry: But you've done great work here. The people might be forbidden to come to you, but they'll not forget what you've done for them. When the cholera epidemic was on them, will they forget your help then?

Rev. Mother. Sister Henry, if what I am planning is successful, we shall leave with the Consul.

Henry. Whatever plans you may have, Reverend Mother, I think it would be better to leave with the Consul. He will be in a difficult position should we stay.

Rev. Mother. Did he ask you to persuade me?

Henry. He did. But you know I agree with him.

(Bridget *enters excitedly up* c)

Bridget (*moving down* c) Reverend Mother! Reverend Mother! There's a great stream of soldiers coming down the road to the Mission. They're stopping at the drive-in.

(Henry *crosses to the window up* lc *and looks out*)

Rev. Mother. Soldiers?

Bridget. And there's an officer in a little car at the gate. Will I go out?

Rev. Mother. No. Better to wait.

Bridget. Sure, they can't eat me, but they'll be after the chickens, maybe. They'd eat *them* all right.

Rev. Mother. They may not be for here at all. Just take a look, then, Sister Bridget.

(Bridget *moves to the door up* c)

(*She rises*) No. I'll go myself.

(*The* Reverend Mother *exits up* c)

Bridget. Has the Consul fellah gone?

Henry (*crossing to the table*) He has, but he's returning. His wife is staying here. (*She sorts the books on the table*)

Bridget. She looks a fast one all right.

Henry. That's not a charitable remark, Sister Bridget.

Bridget (*unperturbed*) Maybe not, but it's true. Mind, I didn't say she *was* fast. Do you think the soldiers have come to whip us off?

Henry. The Consul says we are to leave on the boat in a day or so. He has permission for us to go.

Bridget. Then it's off we'll be all right. (*She moves down* l)

Poor Reverend Mother and Sister Magdalen. They've been here so long.

HENRY. And what would be the use of us staying, anyway, and Father Schiller arrested, too.

BRIDGET. They've taken him? (*She sits on the chair* L) God have mercy on him. Why would they arrest a fine man like that? Is it the General has done it?

HENRY. Who else? Isn't he the Governor?

BRIDGET (*upset*) But this is a dreadful thing for Sister Magdalen and her the General's godmother. She'll die if she hears. We'll not tell her. 'Twould break the poor soul's heart.

HENRY. She'll find out sooner or later.

(*The* REVEREND MOTHER *enters up* C. BRIDGET *rises*)

REV. MOTHER (*calling through the doorway*) In here, Captain Lee. (*She moves* RC)

(CAPTAIN LEE *enters up* C. *He wears the uniform of a Communist Army Captain. He is a tall man of about thirty-five. He has a hard-bitten face and an offhand manner. He is an Englishman and speaks with a London accent*)

(*She eyes Lee with distaste*) This is Captain Lee. He has some instructions for us.

LEE. Not instructions. (*He leans against the door post*) I wanted to make sure you know how things stand. No need for any trouble.

BRIDGET. Faith! It's an Englishman you are. What in·the name of God are you doing in that outfit? Are you a spy, then?

LEE. Never mind my uniform. I've come to tip you off—your pal has escaped.

HENRY. What do you mean?

LEE. The Jerry—Father Schiller.

BRIDGET (*delighted*) He's got away? That's grand news!

LEE (*crossing to Bridget*) Not for long it won't be. When we do catch up with him he'll wish he'd sat tight in his cell. (*He crosses to* L *of the table*) The point is, we shouldn't be surprised if he makes a bee-line here when things quieten down. So we're putting a guard round the place.

REV. MOTHER. We're supposed to be leaving in a day or so.

LEE. So they tell me, and until you go the guards stay put. Don't worry, you won't get hurt—providing you keep in line.

HENRY. We knew nothing of Father Schiller's arrest until the Consul was after telling us today. His wife is staying here.

LEE. Then you knew he'd escaped?

HENRY. We didn't even know he'd been arrested, until today. I just told you. Why would they arrest him, anyway?

LEE (*with a wry smile*) He's been charged with acting as a spy for the Imperialist Powers against the People's Republic.

REV. MOTHER. What nonsense!

LEE. It's damned impressive nonsense, though, and gets you shot out here. Well, I'll be seeing you from time to time. I'll inspect the place later—just a formality, and of course we'll escort you on to the boat. (*He smiles*) Just in case you try and smuggle any secret documents out to the Imperialists.

BRIDGET. You ought to be ashamed of yourself, an Englishman acting like this.

LEE (*sharply*) Cut it out! As far as you're concerned I'm a Captain in the People's Republican Army who speaks English—and understands Irish—(*he moves to the door up* C) and I'm taking one of your chickens for dinner.

BRIDGET (*crossing to Lee*) You leave them chickens alone.

LEE. There's a white cockerel there will do me nicely.

BRIDGET. Why you . . .

REV. MOTHER (*interrupting*) Be quiet now, Bridget. (*To Lee*) Thank you, Captain—and it's very welcome you are to a chicken.

LEE (*sarcastically*) Thank *you*. (*He goes on to the verandah*)

(BRIDGET *slams the door behind Lee*)

(*He looks in at the window up* LC. *Harshly*) And if that Boche should get past my guard, I want to know. Not that I think he will. My men are good—trained 'em meself. Good shots—remember that.

(LEE *exits* L *on the verandah*)

BRIDGET (*moving down* L) For two pins I'd take the kitchen knife to him. What's he doing, soldiering with that lot?

REV. MOTHER (*moving up* C; *wearily*) Sister Bridget, quiet please—I want to think. (*She looks out of the window up* RC)

HENRY. So Father Schiller has escaped. He'd never get through to here, Reverend Mother.

REV. MOTHER. He came here in the early hours of this morning. (*She turns*)

BRIDGET (*moving* C) What!

HENRY (*moving to* L *of the table*) Why didn't you tell us then?

REV. MOTHER. I wanted to keep it to myself as long as possible. He's in the dormitory of the school—I want him away from Mrs Stilton.

HENRY. You gave her his room.

REV. MOTHER. I couldn't be putting her in the dormitory.

BRIDGET. And they're sitting outside waiting for the Father to come. What a laugh.

HENRY. There will be little to laugh at if they search the Mission.

REV. MOTHER. It was my idea to get him away before we'd leave here.

HENRY. And that's why you had no certainty about going. (*Suddenly*) Oh, Reverend Mother, I'm sorry for the things I've said.

REV. MOTHER. Think no more of it, Sister Henry, you were

not to know the reason I had. I'd perhaps have been better telling you all—but to my mind I thought it was better to say nothing for a while.

BRIDGET. Would we be able to take him with us?

REV. MOTHER. They'll see us on to the boat—and then there is the Consul.

HENRY. And his wife. She has no love for Father Schiller—although the only reason she'd give is him being German. She certainly mustn't find out he's here.

REV. MOTHER. Now can we leave him? The poor man can hardly walk.

BRIDGET. Has he sprained an ankle, then?

REV. MOTHER (*with emotion*) They left him hanging by his feet. (*She moves and sits* L *of the table*)

BRIDGET. Oh, God!

REV. MOTHER. He had to ride here in an ox-cart. But he can barely stand for his swollen ankles. Now we must tell Sister Lucy, but I want Magdalen to know nothing of this. Do you understand me?

HENRY. Was it the General tortured him?

(*The* REVEREND MOTHER *nods her head*)

BRIDGET. Ah, sure we'll find a way out for him. We've a couple of days yet.

HENRY. Unless they search the Mission right away and find him. We must head off this Captain Lee or whatever he calls himself. Perhaps if we were more conciliatory to the man.

BRIDGET. I'd like to crack him on the head with a shillelagh.

HENRY (*acidly*) That would be a great help.

REV. MOTHER. We'll think on it. Meanwhile, guard your tongues before Mrs Stilton.

(MAGDALEN *enters down* L. *There is an awkward silence*)

MAGDALEN (*crossing to the Reverend Mother*) Oh, it's here you all are. Reverend Mother, Sister Lucy says we have a visitor on us. Will I serve a special sweet? Some stewed fruit, I was thinking.

REV. MOTHER (*judicially*) Yes. Yes, I think stewed fruit would be very nice indeed.'

MAGDALEN. The stove is doing fine since you looked at it. (*She crosses to the door* L, *then stops and turns*) I've been thinking on that letter to Peter. I might add a postscript. I remember well at his confirmation I gave him a relic of the Little Flower. I'll ask him if he has it still. If he hasn't I'll send him mine. He'd never lose the faith entirely while he had a relic of the Little Flower.

REV. MOTHER (*with an effort*) Yes. Yes, do.

(MAGDALEN *smiles and exits* L. BRIDGET *bursts unashamedly into tears*)

Now, Sister Bridget!

BRIDGET. She couldn't have loved him more if he'd been her own son. (*Passionately*) What sort of a man can he be to do that to a great woman the like of herself?

HENRY (*moving to the window up* R; *sadly*) I doubt if he even remembers her.

(*There is a momentary silence.*
RUTH *enters down* L)

RUTH. Sorry if I'm butting in on anything, but I haven't any soap. I'd like to tidy up.

BRIDGET. I'll get some for you.

(BRIDGET *exits down* L)

RUTH. It's apparently packed in my trunks, and they're at the barracks. (*She moves to the window up* LC) What are the soldiers doing here?

REV. MOTHER. They came and discussed our leaving on the boat.

RUTH. It looks as though they're going to give you a guard of honour. I hope they don't give a salute as we go. They're rotten shots—I wouldn't like them to sink the damned steamer.

REV. MOTHER. Are you comfortable, Mrs Stilton?

RUTH (*moving towards the door* L) Very. Father Schiller's bed is better than mine at the Consulate—he must have been an honoured guest.

REV. MOTHER. I'm glad you're well settled.

(BRIDGET *enters down* L, *carrying a tablet of soap*)

BRIDGET. Here it is for you.

RUTH (*taking the soap*) Thank you. As a matter of fact there *is* some soap in my room, but it's shaving soap. (*She moves to the door* L *and turns*) I suppose none of you were bearded ladies in an earlier vocation—the soap was wet.

RUTH *exits* L. *The* NUNS *look uneasily at each other as—*

the CURTAIN *falls*

ACT II

Scene 1

SCENE—*The same. The evening of the same day.*

When the CURTAIN *rises, it is dark outside. The doors are closed and the lamps are lit. A large trunk or hamper is down* LC *with a pile of books beside it.* BRIDGET *is at the shelves up* L, *taking books from them to pack in the trunk. She sings as she brings a pile of books and adds them to the pile* R *of the trunk.* LUCY *enters* L *and crosses to* L *of the trunk.*

LUCY. Will I give you a hand, Sister Bridget?

BRIDGET. Sure, Sister Lucy. (*In a hushed voice*) Is she still in her room?

LUCY. Mrs Stilton, do you mean? Sure, she went straight away there when we finished the meal. She has little to say for herself.

BRIDGET. I'd say she's after knowin' that Father Schiller is here. (*She packs some books*)

LUCY (*crossing to the shelves up* R) She said nothing of it. (*She takes some books from the shelves*)

BRIDGET. And how could she? I mean, she couldn't say out like "I think it's a priest you've got hidden about the place". And if you'd heard the way she said about the soap!

LUCY (*crossing to the trunk*) It's no concern of the woman, anyway. (*She adds her books to the pile* R *of the trunk*)

BRIDGET. Sister Henry says she has a great dislike of Father Schiller on account of his being a German.

LUCY. We'll know soon enough. (*She crosses to the shelves up* R)

BRIDGET (*packing books*) That Captain fellah says he's coming to look over the Mission tonight. Be the look of the man he'd enjoy nothing more than filling the lot of us with bullets. And Sister Henry says we should be conciliatory.

LUCY (*taking books from the shelves*) Sure it would be a bad thing to upset the man. Do you say he was an *Englishman*?

BRIDGET. Surely he was. Why any minute he'd be doing the *Lambeth Walk* for you. He's as English as the Archbishop of Canterbury. May God forgive them both.

LUCY (*crossing to the trunk*) Well now, it seems a strange thing altogether. Would he have a Chinese mother? (*She adds her books to the pile* R *of the trunk and returns to the shelves up* R)

BRIDGET. If he had a Chinese mother, so did St Patrick.

(HENRY *enters* L *and crosses to* C)

HENRY (*eyeing their activities with disfavour*) What are you at with the books?

BRIDGET. Reverend Mother says for us to look ready to leave. It would look less suspicious, she says.

HENRY. I intended to make a list of those books. Are you putting them in the trunk in any sort of order?

BRIDGET. Sure. We're putting the big ones at the bottom.

HENRY (*irritably*) That's a great help to me. How will I know where anything is when I come to unpack?

LUCY (*crossing to* R *of Bridget*) I'd say it isn't of great importance, Sister Henry.

HENRY. I'm in charge of the library and I'd say it was of great importance. (*Suddenly weary*) Oh, do what you will with them. (*She crosses to* R *of the table*)

BRIDGET. We've put only a few in there, Sister Henry. We'll have them out in the flick of a cow's tail. Here, Sister Lucy. (*She dives into the trunk and fishes out some books*)

HENRY (*mollified*) It would be better.

(BRIDGET *takes the books to the shelves up* R)

I may have time for them myself in the morning. Did the Officer come yet?

LUCY. We've not seen him. He's put a string of soldiers all round the Mission. Heaven knows how we'd get Father Schiller away through the lot of them. I'll talk to Ling Hu about it later. He'd surely know some way to smuggle the poor man out through the guard.

BRIDGET (*crossing to the trunk*) He's a clever one all right, is Ling Hu. (*She collects some books and takes them to the shelves up* R) All them Buddhists is like that. They're as full of answers as a penny catechism.

HENRY. If it's help you want to give me, the books in the schoolroom are all listed. We could pack them in cases. (*She moves to* R *of the trunk*)

LUCY. Sure, we'll do it before dark. (*She moves to* L *of Henry*) Is Reverend Mother with—(*quietly*) Father Schiller?

HENRY. She is.

(RUTH *enters down* L *and crosses to* L *of the trunk. She is smoking a cigarette*)

Can we do anything for you, Mrs Stilton?

RUTH (*glancing around*) Do I see some books?

BRIDGET. We've just been packing and unpacking them. Help yourself.

HENRY. If you'll excuse us we've some more packing to do— some books in the schoolroom.

RUTH. And then do you unpack them again? Is it some sort of religious exercise?

(BRIDGET *crosses to* R *of Ruth*)

HENRY. We just want to be ready to leave.

Scene 1   A LETTER FROM THE GENERAL   23

RUTH. Has the Reverend Mother decided to listen to you, then?
HENRY. It's well to be prepared for any eventuality.
RUTH. Like Boy Scouts—or Girl Guides. Is there anything to drink in the Mission?
BRIDGET. Only water.
RUTH. No, thank you.
BRIDGET. It's been boiled.
RUTH. That sounds even less attractive. Thanks all the same. By the way, congratulate the Sister who does the cooking. A most enjoyable meal. Now, don't you bother about me, I'll just browse among the books.
HENRY. I doubt if you'll find anything . . . (*She breaks off*)
RUTH (*smiling*) You imply that it's all elevating literature. Surely that's just what I need?
BRIDGET. I've an Agatha Christie up in my room if you'd like it.
RUTH. Don't tempt me, Sister Bridget. Give me a chance to be elevated.

(HENRY, LUCY *and* BRIDGET *exit up* C. RUTH *wanders to the shelves up* R, *looks at the titles of the books with expressions of dismay, crosses to the shelves up* LC, *takes out a book, looks at the titles and raises her eyebrows. There is a knock on the door up* C.

LEE *enters up* C)

(*She looks up from the book*) Good God!
LEE. 'Evening. I suppose you're Mrs Stilton, the Consul's wife. Heard you were here.
RUTH. If I hadn't been gasping for a drink for the past three hours I'd say I was seeing and hearing things. Who are you? Chu Chin Chow?
LEE. You make jokes, I see. I'm Captain Lee of the People's Republican Army.
RUTH (*crossing to the table*) With that uniform and that voice I thought you were part of an Amateur Theatrical Show.
LEE. Very funny! (*He moves* C) The Reverend Mother about?
RUTH. I don't know. She may be in her room. I'm not familiar with the routine here. Three of the nuns were packing and unpacking books. (*She sits in the armchair* RC)
LEE (*wandering around*) Lots of books here.
RUTH. I don't think most of them would pass your political censor. What do you want the Reverend Mother for? Are you going to shoot her?
LEE (*turning to Ruth; harshly*) If I'm ordered to shoot her, she'll be shot.
RUTH. You're a sort of proletarian Heath Robinson, aren't you? Pardon my curiosity, but how do you get mixed up in the People's Republican Army? If you're a disciple of Karl Marx couldn't you get work nearer home—starting railway strikes or that sort of thing?

LEE (*moving and perching on the downstage edge of the table*) You're full of funny sayings, aren't you, Mrs Stilton? (*Sharply*) Don't try and take a rise out of me. You're not at a garden party at Buckingham Palace.

RUTH. You seem to have a misplaced idea of where Consuls' wives come in the social scale. You didn't tell me how you came by that uniform. You're sure you're not an M.I.5 man in disguise?

LEE. I'm a soldier, Mrs Stilton—that's why I wear this uniform. I'm a bloody good soldier, too.

RUTH. I see. When you left school you had your calling-up papers and reported to the Far East.

LEE. I left school when I was fourteen. If I'd stayed at some Public School until I was seventeen I might have been made a Captain in the British Army.

RUTH. I somehow didn't think you were an old Etonian.

LEE. I suppose I'd be a lot better man if I was. (*He takes a flask from his pocket and drinks*) Want a drink?

RUTH (*rising and crossing to* C) I don't think so.

LEE. It's whisky.

RUTH. I'm more concerned about where it comes from than what it is.

LEE (*rising; menacingly*) Don't try me too far, Mrs Stilton—I'm only an officer here, they don't make you an officer and a gentleman. (*He spits and stamps it into the floor*)

RUTH. You sound like an unsuccessful candidate for the War Office Selection Board—or did they forget to give you any medals?

(LEE *takes another drink, wipes his mouth on the back of his hand then crosses to* R *of Ruth*)

LEE. Medals! I've got medals! Heard of the D.C.M.? I've got that. The M.M.? I've got that. I've been three times mentioned in dispatches. I told you, I'm a good soldier.

(RUTH *moves up* L)

But don't kid yourself, Mrs Stilton—medals don't mean a bloody thing in the British Army—it's where you went to school that counts.

RUTH. Isn't that rather out of date?

LEE. It's out of date in theory, but try it for yourself. (*He moves to* L *of the table and leans on it*) You can take a rise out of the People's Republican Army but there's only one thing that counts here—can you do your job? No kids with wet nappies from Sandhurst to be carried about.

RUTH (*moving down* LC) I'm still terribly interested to hear how you came to join.

LEE. I was captured in Malaya and offered a job—or have me head lopped off. They had an answer in half a minute—I took the job.

Scene 1 A LETTER FROM THE GENERAL

RUTH (*sardonically*) You gave the matter a great deal of thought.

LEE. I was eating when they asked me—as soon as my mouth was empty I said "Yes".

RUTH. And now you go about shooting nuns, and English soldiers I've no doubt.

LEE. Whatever side I'm on, I'm a good soldier. The enemy is the other side.

RUTH. A renegade is more apt, don't you think?

LEE. Not at all. I'm a soldier and I fight for whoever pays me best, and where I get the best opportunities to do my job. (*Blandly*) I'm what they used to call a mercenary—it's a trade. Do you know how many times the King of England kept the throne using mercenaries?

RUTH (*sitting on the trunk*) I was never any good at history.

LEE. I wasn't bad meself. In fact, I'm good at anything I set me mind to. (*He drinks*) But take my tip—if you've got any kids keep 'em out of the Services in England, unless you can pull a few strings.

RUTH (*suddenly angry*) Thank you for your advice, but you're a little too late. My son was killed in the war.

LEE (*unmoved*) Hard luck.

RUTH (*rising and turning on him*) Damned good luck if he'd been going to turn out like you.

LEE (*calmly*) Don't take it out on me. I was in the war meself. Did the kid get any medals?

RUTH. He won the D.F.C. and Bar . . . (*She breaks off and weeps*)

LEE. Sorry and all that but I never shot him down. Anyway, the R.A.F. is different. They go more on what you can do than who you are.

RUTH (*viciously*) Oh, shut up!

LEE (*unperturbed*) You started it. If you must take the rise out of people don't get upset when it bounces back on you. You want to take it out on the people who shot him down—not me.

RUTH (*almost to herself*) He wasn't shot down—he was shot in the back, trying to escape.

LEE. The Jerries?

RUTH. Yes. The swine.

LEE. They wasn't too fussy. I'm after one of the bastards now.

RUTH. What do you mean?

LEE. A priest. "Schiller" his name is. He's escaped. It's a dead cert he'll make for this place. I've got guards all round it.

RUTH. You mean he's escaped from the prison at the Capital?

LEE. That's right. One of the guards was an old Mission school kid. Got him out. But he won't get far. I'm just giving the place the once over. Make sure there's no way he can slip in here.

RUTH (*moving* C; *thoughtfully*) I suppose it hasn't occurred to you that he might already be here?

LEE (*rising; alert*) You've seen him? These nuns have said something?
RUTH (*crossing below the table*) Not a word. But I've an idea it wouldn't hurt to give the place a thorough search. I may be wrong.
LEE. Well, thanks. (*He crosses to* LC) I'll have to tread a bit careful. I've had orders to use kid gloves as long as they behave themselves. Are you sure he's here?
RUTH. Not at all. I just found a wet shaving stick in my room —and it was his room when he stayed here.
LEE (*thoughtfully*) Wet shaving stick? Could have fallen in a basin or something. Not much to go on. (*He crosses to* L *of Ruth*) But if he's here I'll smell him out.
RUTH. I'm sure you will. Where are you camping?
LEE. By the gate. End of the driveway.

(LUCY *enters up* C)

LUCY (*giving Lee an odd look*) I'm sorry.
RUTH. The Captain wants to see the Reverend Mother, Sister.
LUCY. Sure. I'll away and get her.

(LUCY *exits down* L)

LEE (*looking after Lucy*) Didn't see her this afternoon.
RUTH. Didn't you? Did you see the old one? Sister Magdalen, I think she is. You'd get on well with her. She's General Mei Cheng's godmother.
LEE (*crossing to* C) You're being funny again.
RUTH. Not me. She told me herself. And she's not the leg-pulling type.
LEE. You mean Mei Cheng went to a Mission School? This one? (*He whistles*)
RUTH. I don't think it was this one, but he seems to have been Sister Magdalen's prize pupil.
LEE. Well, I'm damned! That accounts for the kid gloves order. He certainly wants them out of here quickly with no trouble.
RUTH. I think it's rather intriguing. I always thought the General was a man of steel.

(HENRY *enters up* C, *crosses and exits down* L)

LEE. He is, but he wants Schiller. (*He pauses*) I think I've got it.
RUTH. What?
LEE. If the General gets Schiller nicely shot and buried, there won't be any kick about a few nuns getting away. Close the Mission. Kill the visiting priest, a Jerry that no-one is going to bother about—deport the nuns. Yes. It won't look too bad on is record. But Schiller has gummed it up by escaping.
RUTH (*moving to* R *of Lee*) I think if you want promotion in the

Scene 1 A LETTER FROM THE GENERAL

People's Republican Army, you'd better get Schiller for your General.

(*The* REVEREND MOTHER *enters* L. *She eyes* RUTH *and* LEE *closely as they stand together*)

REV. MOTHER. You were wanting to see me, Captain Lee?
LEE. That's right.
REV. MOTHER. I am at your disposal.
RUTH (*crossing below the Reverend Mother to the door* L) If you'll excuse me. I just came down for a book.
REV. MOTHER. I hope you found one to your taste, Mrs Stilton.
RUTH. I've taken this. *The Thing*, by Chesterton.
REV. MOTHER. They'd be essays. You should find them entertaining.
RUTH. The title fascinated me. It's something I've never quite been. (*To Lee*) Good hunting.

(RUTH *exits* L)

LEE (*moving and sitting above the table*) Sit down, Reverend Mother. I'd like to ask you a few questions.
REV. MOTHER (*ironically*) Thank you. (*She crosses and sits* L *of the table*) What did you want to know?
LEE. You know I'm looking for Father Schiller?
REV. MOTHER. You said so earlier.
LEE. I've got an idea. (*He pauses*)

(*The* REVEREND MOTHER *looks questioningly at Lee*)

I'm sitting outside the Mission waiting for him to come. Then I get this idea that he might be here inside all the time.
REV. MOTHER. And why would you think a thing like that?
LEE. Just a hunch. Is he here?
REV. MOTHER. If Father Schiller were in the Mission, I'd surely know about it.
LEE. That's why I'm asking you. Is he?
REV. MOTHER. No.
LEE. I hope you're not telling me lies, Reverend Mother.
REV. MOTHER. Thank you.
LEE. Don't misunderstand me. I wouldn't expect the truth under the circumstances. So it's no reflection on your character. Suppose I take a look round the place.
REV. MOTHER. Thank you for . . .
LEE (*rising; interrupting*) Cut the sarcasm. Just let me tell you how you stand. If Schiller's here he can't get out. In two days you'll be on that boat. So you'll leave him behind. So then I come into the place and tear it apart until I find him. Then I get after the boat and you'll be brought back and shot. (*He pauses*) What'll happen to you before they shoot you I wouldn't like to say. So think about it, and if he's here I advise you to tell me for the sake of your nuns.

REV. MOTHER (*rising and moving* C) Was it General Mei Cheng who sent you here?
LEE. It was. And let me tell you, to get Father Schiller he'd shoot his own mother, let alone his godmother. Our Government aren't fond of Governors who let prisoners escape.
REV. MOTHER. I'm sorry, but I can't help you, Captain Lee.
LEE (*moving to* R *of the table*) Pity. Save us both a lot of trouble. I don't like causing trouble for anyone.
REV. MOTHER. Your conscience disturbs you?
LEE. Not a bit. I just like things to be tidy.
REV. MOTHER. It's sorry for you I am.
LEE (*turning angrily on her*) I don't want that sort of yap. (*He crosses to* R *of her*) I'm doing my job and I like my job so you can cut out any bloody pious thought about my conscience.

(BRIDGET *enters up* C)

BRIDGET (*moving down* RC) Reverend Mother . . .
LEE (*cutting in*) I don't want any of you talking to the Reverend Mother. Tell the rest of the nuns to come here.
BRIDGET. Now, Captain?
LEE. No! Next Christmas! Go on, and have them here in two minutes.
BRIDGET. I see that chicken never choked you, then?
REV. MOTHER. Bridget!

(BRIDGET *crosses and exits* L)

LEE (*moving above the table*) You'll all stay here while I take a look round. I won't call the soldiers in yet. When I've done, they can search the grounds and God help your priest if they find him.
REV. MOTHER. What harm has Father Schiller ever done you, Captain Lee, that you're so vicious towards the poor man?
LEE. Apart from being a priest, which doesn't make him popular with my bosses, he's a Jerry, which doesn't make him popular with me.
REV. MOTHER (*thoughtfully*) I see. And did Mrs Stilton tell you why she has a dislike of Germans?
LEE. They put a bullet through her boy's back when he was escaping from a prison camp.
REV. MOTHER. The poor woman.
LEE. There's a lot of poor women feel like her about Jerries.
REV. MOTHER. War is a terrible thing for us all, but sometimes the poison left after is worse.
LEE. Schiller is one bit of poison that's going to be wiped out.
REV. MOTHER. Father Schiller was here all through the war.
LEE. I know—and the fact the Japs never interned him doesn't win him any medals with Mei Cheng.
REV. MOTHER. Germany was an ally of Japan.
LEE. Save your breath. (*He moves below the table*) I'm not interested in the International Situation.

Scene 1   A LETTER FROM THE GENERAL   29

REV. MOTHER. If you were to know the great work Father Schiller did for the wretched people interned by the Japanese, you might have some sympathy for him. I was one of them and what we'd have done without him I don't know.

LEE. I know what I shall do with him when I get him.

(HENRY, BRIDGET *and* LUCY *enter* L. BRIDGET *stands* L *of the Reverend Mother.* HENRY *and* LUCY *stand down* L)

Where's the other one?

HENRY. Sister Magdalen is in bed. She's very old and takes to her bed early. I didn't want to rouse her unless the matter was greatly important.

LEE. She's the one who's the General's godmother, isn't she?

REV. MOTHER. Yes.

LEE. I want you to stay here—all of you. Do you give me your word to stay in this room? Then I'll let the old one have her beauty sleep. I suppose Father Schiller isn't under her bed?

BRIDGET. Father Schiller? You . . . (*She breaks off*)

LEE (*crossing to Bridget; keenly*) Yes?

(BRIDGET *is silent*)

You were going to say something about Father Schiller? (*He turns suddenly to the Reverend Mother*) I want you to come on the verandah with me, Reverend Mother. (*He moves up* C *and waits at the door*)

(*The* REVEREND MOTHER *exits up* C.

LEE *follows her off. The* NUNS *look at one another and are about to speak.* BRIDGET *moves up* C.

LEE *re-enters. The* NUNS *stand watching* LEE *as he moves* RC *and eyes them*)

BRIDGET. What have you sent Reverend Mother out there for?

LEE. I thought it would be easier for her. She's only just outside.

HENRY. Easier for her?

LEE. I explained to the Reverend Mother that if she didn't tell me whether Father Schiller was here or not I would have to arrest you all. (*He moves* LC) You know what that means.

BRIDGET. You must have talked as fast as lightning.

LEE. I didn't tell her just now, but before you came in. She was sensible enough to tell me he was here.

BRIDGET. She told you . . . ?

HENRY (*quickly*) And why would she say a thing like that?

LEE. Because he is, that's why. But her conscience pulled her up short. She didn't tell me exactly where he was. To save turning the place upside down perhaps one of you would go and fetch him for me. It would be better if the Reverend Mother didn't see me take him. You can keep out of it, too. Just tell him he's wanted in this room. He'll come if one of you tell him.

(*The* NUNS *do not move or speak*)

(*Harshly*) Go on! (*He moves to* R *of Bridget*) You've most to say. You go.

BRIDGET. I'd have a lot more to say only for me being what I am. Just for two minutes I'm wishing I was a farm girl again.

LEE. Cut the cackle and get Schiller. I know he's here and you'll save everybody a lot of trouble by getting him to come quietly.

HENRY (*to Lucy*) It occurs to me that the strain of being cooped up here has upset Reverend Mother. Whatever would make her think Father Schiller was here in the Mission?

LUCY. God alone can say, Sister Henry. Did you hear herself speak of Father Schiller, Sister Bridget?

BRIDGET. She was saying what a terrible thing it was him being arrested—(*with a sidelong glance at Lee*) but them poor heathens don't know any better.

LEE. Very nice. (*He moves below the table, takes out his flask and drinks*)

HENRY. It seems we can't help you, Captain Lee. You seem to be under a misapprehension. As far as we know, Father Schiller is not in the building. Would you look for yourself, perhaps?

LEE (*savagely*) I'll look all right. You won't put me off with that damned nonsense. (*He crosses to the door* L *and turns*) Stay here until I come back—and any time you choose to disobey my orders I'll fill the place with soldiers to enforce them. And my soldiers aren't Mission boys. So take my tip and stay put.

(LEE *exits* L, *slamming the door behind him. There is a silence*)

LUCY. I sent him back to the shed. I said we'd signal from the verandah when Lee had taken himself off.

BRIDGET (*moving* C) But there's two soldiers be the fence right opposite the shed.

HENRY (*moving to the door up* C) I'll take a look.

BRIDGET. They'll clap eyes on you if you go round to the shed.

HENRY. Sure, if you could see the soldiers so could Father Schiller. Were they inside the fence or outside? (*She moves to the window up* LC)

BRIDGET. They was outside, but they snoop about like foxes.

HENRY (*peering out of the window; softly*) Reverend Mother.

BRIDGET. Is it on the verandah she is?

HENRY. No, she's gone. (*She moves to the door up* C)

LUCY. I wouldn't go out there, Sister Henry. Sure, he couldn't have harmed her, he wasn't with her a second.

HENRY. I'm going to see for myself.

BRIDGET. So am I.

LUCY. And if the officer comes back and you not here he'll have the soldiers in and destroy the place.

HENRY. He might well have called a soldier to take Reverend Mother off.

LUCY. Ah, sure we'd have heard him. He wasn't . . .

(*The* REVEREND MOTHER *enters up* C)

BRIDGET (*with a gush of relief*) Ah, Reverend Mother. We're just after thinking you were arrested or something terrible.

REV. MOTHER. Where is Captain Lee?

HENRY. He'd have us believe you told him Father Schiller was here. He tried to make us say where he was hidden. Sister Lucy sent Father Schiller to the back of the shed—but Sister Bridget is feared the soldiers will see him.

REV. MOTHER. They might. (*She looks towards the door up* C) Father Schiller is on the verandah now. He saw me come out there with the Captain. Now, if we can get the Captain to leave by the side door . . .

(*Suddenly shouts in a foreign tongue are heard off up* C. *The* NUNS *all look towards the door up* C *as it opens.*

FATHER SCHILLER *enters up* C. *He is aged fifty, but his tired, haggard appearance makes him seem older. He walks badly, and wears a torn, soiled white habit. He speaks with a German accent*)

Father!

SCHILLER. The soldiers outside. I was afraid they would see me.

REV. MOTHER. They'll not come in here yet, the Captain isn't sure of himself.

HENRY (*leading Schiller to the chair* L *of the table*) Sit yourself down, Father. (*To Bridget*) Watch for the Captain in the corridor.

(SCHILLER *sinks on to the chair.* BRIDGET *runs to the door* L, *opens it a little and watches for Lee*)

SCHILLER. Reverend Mother—I think it would be best for me to give myself up to this man. Then you and the Sisters will have no trouble.

HENRY. He'll trouble us whatever happens. I'm only hoping he'll leave Sister Magdalen in peace.

LUCY. Sure, it would take an earthquake to wake her.

REV. MOTHER. I see no reason for you to give yourself up, Father. We might well be able to smuggle you out yet. The Captain isn't at all certain you're here.

LUCY. That's true. He'd burn the place down if he was.

SCHILLER. He is an Englishman, you say? This Captain?

LUCY. He has the appearance of one, but I'd say he was more like a head-hunter.

REV. MOTHER. Sister Lucy, will you just go out on to the verandah and without attracting attention see if those soldiers are still in sight.

(LUCY *nods and exits up* C)

SCHILLER. I cannot understand why we should be treated so. We do no harm—and now my coming has brought this new trouble upon you.

HENRY. I tell you, Father, the trouble will come to us, anyway. I'd say the Captain is only letting us alone to be bait for you. I doubt we'll ever see that steamer.

REV. MOTHER. The Consul has arranged it.

HENRY. I'd not rely too much on him. And what with the way his wife feels about Father Schiller he'll not strain himself to help us.

SCHILLER. Does this woman know me? She has a dislike for me?

REV. MOTHER. It's not a personal dislike, Father. Her son was shot and killed escaping from a German prison camp—she has a great bitterness towards all Germans.

(SCHILLER *nods understandingly*)

HENRY. It would have been her told the Captain you were here, Father.

SCHILLER. She knows I am here?

REV. MOTHER. She said something which gave us to think she'd guessed as much.

BRIDGET. And Sister Lucy saw her talking to the Captain a while back.

HENRY. She can't be sure, any more than the Captain.

(LUCY *enters up* C)

LUCY (*moving down* L) They're still out there—but they've moved themselves over by the chicken compound. What'll we do if the Captain comes back in here?

HENRY (*to Bridget*) Is the passage clear?

(BRIDGET *looks off* L *and nods*)

Then why wouldn't we put him in the cupboard out there in the corridor?

REV. MOTHER. And if he looks in the cupboard on his way back?

HENRY. We must take a chance. There isn't a place we can be certain he hasn't searched.

REV. MOTHER. There is, indeed. This room. Why would he search here?

HENRY. How could we hide Father in here?

(*They look around the room*)

REV. MOTHER. The cupboard.

(*They look at the cupboard*)

LUCY. We'd never get the junk out from there in time. We should ask St Anthony to find a hiding place for us. (*She wanders around*)

BRIDGET. St Anthony?

LUCY. Sure, if he's good at finding things, he'd be right clever at hiding them. (*She suddenly knocks against the trunk*) There! What did I say? He's done it! The trunk!

Scene 1   A LETTER FROM THE GENERAL

(*The others exchange doubtful glances*)

Rev. Mother. Could you get in there, Father? It's terribly cramped you'd be.

Schiller (*wryly*) I have been more uncomfortable recently. (*He rises*)

Rev. Mother (*decisively*) Quickly, then.

(*The* Reverend Mother, Lucy *and* Henry *help* Schiller *into the trunk*)

How is it, Father?

Schiller. It will be well enough—only for my feet—they hurt a little.

Bridget (*from the door* L) Quickly—shut the lid. He's coming now, with the Consul's wife.

(Henry *closes the lid and moves down* R. Lucy *goes up* L. *The* Reverend Mother *makes a hurried sign of the cross, then sits* L *of the table.* Bridget *crosses to* L *of the Reverend Mother*)

Rev. Mother. Keep your eyes from the trunk, all of you.

(Lee *enters* L.
Ruth *follows him on*)

Ruth. I think you might have told the Captain which was my room. He seems to think Father Schiller is here—I've been helping him to search.

Henry. I hope you didn't wake Sister Magdalen.

Ruth. No. I showed him her room and he watched me look round there.

Henry. You didn't find Father Schiller, then, Captain?

Lee. No. But you'll have a job to keep him tucked away—now I've got Mrs Stilton to keep an eye on things for me.

Henry. I can't see why Mrs Stilton should be so certain he is here.

Ruth. Oh, I'm not—but it's fun finding out.

Lee (*moving to the cupboard*) You're going to be sorry if you've made a fool of me. What's in here?

Lucy (*her voice trembling as she realizes he is about to search the room*) Sure, just a lot of old junk, Captain.

Lee. Not old German junk?

Rev. Mother. I shouldn't bother to open that, Captain, you can take my word it's . . .

(Lee *pulls the cupboard door violently open and the junk tumbles out all over his feet*)

Ruth (*smiling*) Sort it out, Captain—he might be underneath.

Lee (*feeling foolish; angrily*) Shut your trap!

(Lee *wanders up* c, *then down* lc. *The* Nuns *watch him tensely as he passes the trunk. Suddenly he turns and kicks it*)

RUTH. The books can't fall out of there on you, Captain.
LEE. Before you go we'll unpack all these and have a bonfire.
HENRY. You can't burn the truth, Captain. Every despotic regime has burnt books, but the truth lives in the minds of men.

(LEE *bends down to open the trunk*)

BRIDGET (*crossing to* R *of Lee*) Don't waste your breath on him, Sister Henry. The poor man is only an ignorant heathen—how can he read? (*She looks mockingly at Lee*)

(LEE, *with a look of suppressed rage, straightens up and strikes Bridget savagely across the face.* BRIDGET *falls to the floor. The* REVEREND MOTHER *rises*)

REV. MOTHER (*rushing to Bridget*) For God's sake take yourself out of here, Captain Lee.

(LEE *faces them all for a second then turns and stalks out up* C. *The* REVEREND MOTHER *helps* BRIDGET *to her feet*)

My poor child . . .

BRIDGET (*brightly*) It was worth it, Reverend Mother.

REV. MOTHER (*looking at Ruth; coldly*) Is there anything detaining you, Mrs Stilton?

RUTH. Don't pick on me—I'm neutral. (*She moves to the door* L *and turns*) I should tell your German priest to get out of that trunk —he'll get cramp.

(*The others look staggered*)

LUCY. You—you knew he was there?

RUTH. Our friend the Captain wasn't very observant. It was obvious the trunk was full when he kicked it, but not with books. They were on the shelf—as they were when he came in. He didn't deserve to find Father Schiller—not that time.

RUTH *exits* L *as—*

the CURTAIN *falls*

SCENE 2

SCENE—*The same.* The next morning.

When the CURTAIN *rises, the trunk has been removed.* RUTH *is seated in the armchair, reading.* BRIDGET *enters excitedly up* C.

BRIDGET (*moving to* L *of the table*) They've gone. There's not a soul there.

RUTH. Who? The soldiers?

BRIDGET (*sitting* L *of the table*) Not at all. Small chance of them going. No, it's the Ling family. Old Ling Hu, his wife and the children. The furniture's gone, too, except for old Ling Hu's bed he took such a pride in.

RUTH. Why the excitement? I expect they've heard you'll be leaving and cleared out.

BRIDGET. But where would they go? I don't understand it at all.

RUTH. Asia is quite a large continent, and it's theirs. I should not go into hysterics, anyway. Who *are* they?

BRIDGET. Sure, they lived in a boat on the river. When their boat was smashed to pieces we let them come here. They took over that hut, do you see.

(HENRY *enters* L *and crosses to* C. BRIDGET *rises and moves to* R *of Henry*)

HENRY. It's here you are, Sister Bridget. Reverend Mother says would you . . .?

BRIDGET (*cutting in*) The Ling family are gone, Sister Henry. I've just been to the hut. Sure, the old man's bed is all that's left there.

HENRY. Where did they go?

RUTH. We don't know. It's a terrific mystery. The suspense is killing me.

HENRY (*sharply*) This happens to be serious for us, Mrs Stilton. (*To Bridget*) You'd better be off and tell Reverend Mother, Sister Bridget. Did you enquire if the soldiers are after seeing them?

BRIDGET. I did not. The less I see of them soldiers, the better it suits me.

(BRIDGET *crosses and exits* L)

RUTH. How is Father Schiller this morning?

HENRY (*moving to* L *of the table*) Not too well.

RUTH. He was lucky last night.

HENRY. God often protects those who serve him well—even Germans.

RUTH. Your sharpness doesn't become your vocation, Sister Henry. You should have a charitable smile for all—even me. And don't forget how embarrassing it would be if Captain Lee were to receive definite information that Father Schiller was here in the Mission. He isn't *quite* certain and he has his orders. But one word from me and he'll tear this place apart.

HENRY. Mrs Stilton, you are in a very strong position. But don't imagine you can ridicule our Mission and be treated as a normal guest. Our work may seem futile, but we have pride in it and if we find ourselves lined up to be shot it will be no more than we've expected for months.

RUTH. You were pretty anxious to get out yesterday.

HENRY. I am still. My vocation doesn't include a yearning to be filled with bullets—but it's an occupational risk—I'm ready for it.

RUTH. Well, you won't be filled with bullets on my account. I've taken a dislike to Captain Lee. He's an impetuous man—he knocks women about—I don't like the type. You can put it down to female prejudice.

(STILTON *enters up* C. *He is looking weary and untidy.* RUTH *rises*)

HENRY (*moving to* R *of Stilton*) Mr Stilton. Good morning to you.

STILTON. Hope I'm not intruding.

HENRY. Of course not. Won't you come right in.

(STILTON *crosses and leans on the downstage edge of the table*)

RUTH. I won't ask you if you had a nice trip, Arthur, you obviously didn't.

STILTON. Hello, Ruth. All that chase and I missed the idiot. I left a letter for him and went to the Capital. They've promised an exit visa for him. What the blazes are all those soldiers doing round the Mission?

HENRY. They've put a guard round us—for fear Father Schiller will come here. Did you know he's after escaping?

STILTON. No, but he's a fool if he has. It'll be a thousand times worse for him when he's taken again. Have you a Sister Magdalen here?

HENRY. We have.

STILTON. I've a letter for her from Mei Cheng.

HENRY (*incredulously*) A letter from the General?

STILTON. Yes. I had to see him about that damned journalist. He asked me to deliver it—didn't want it to come through the army channels.

RUTH. Sister Magdalen is Mei Cheng's godmother.

STILTON. Is she, by George! She ought to be proud of him.

HENRY. You'd favour us, Mr Stilton, if you didn't let Sister Magdalen know too much about the General—and what he's done to the priests and nuns in the Province.

STILTON. Well, she doesn't imagine a Communist General goes about opening church bazaars, does she?

HENRY. Sister Magdalen is very old. She had a great love for the General as a child. She refuses to lose faith in him—she even thinks he might help our cause with the Government.

STILTON. She's an optimist. Still, he's sent this letter through me. It's obviously something personal.

HENRY. You've no idea how it will gladden her heart. Will I take it to her for you?

STILTON. I should prefer to deliver it personally. I promised Mei Cheng I would.

HENRY. I understand. I'll send her to you.

(HENRY *exits* L)

STILTON. Fancy Mei Cheng going soft over a nun. He didn't waste any love on Schiller—grabbed him as soon as he took over here. (*He pauses*) So Schiller's escaped, has he?

RUTH. Yes.
STILTON. And they think he'll come here?
RUTH (*moving to* R *of Stilton*) Apparently.
STILTON. Well, I'm not going to lose any sleep over him. How did you get on here?
RUTH. Oh, I had a riotous time—we played strip poker last night.
STILTON. I hope you haven't been saying things like that to these nuns.
RUTH. Don't worry, they can hold their own when it comes to repartee, especially Sister Henry. Are we leaving on the steamer?
STILTON. Yes. Has the Reverend Mother made up her mind what she wants to do? Not that it makes much difference—Mei Cheng is sending out orders for them to be escorted on to the steamer whether they like it or not. He told me himself.
RUTH. They don't seem to realize how fortunate they are. Did he mention Schiller?
STILTON. No. Why should he? Schiller's not my pigeon. (*He takes out his flask*) Well, tomorrow it's good-bye to this place. (*He drinks*)
RUTH (*holding out her hand for the flask*) I'll drink to that.
STILTON (*handing her the flask*) Do you want a divorce?
RUTH (*moving* R) There doesn't seem much point in going on the way we have been. (*She drinks*)
STILTON. The way you have been, you mean.
RUTH. Of course everything has been my fault.
STILTON. I didn't chase Hutchings and McGregor.
RUTH (*crossing to Stilton and handing him the flask*) If you feel so blameless, would you rather divorce me? (*She crosses below Stilton to* LC) Although I'd remind you there are other things which break up marriages besides Hutchingses and McGregors.

(STILTON *looks at her as though to make an angry reply, then pauses and perches on the table*)

STILTON. Perhaps we married too young. (*Bitterly*) Sometimes I think of the way we planned things were going to be when Bobbie came out of the Air Force.
RUTH (*harshly*) He didn't come out. (*Suddenly*) Arthur—they've got that German priest here.
STILTON (*jumping up*) Schiller! Here, in the Mission?
RUTH. The Captain in charge of the soldiers came here last night. He searched the place but didn't find him.
STILTON. And he was here all the time?
RUTH. Yes. I wasn't sure at the time, but I am now.
STILTON (*angrily*) They must give him up. How on earth did he get past the guards?
RUTH. He was here when they came. He was here when we arrived yesterday.
STILTON. So that's why the Reverend Mother didn't want to

leave. She knew they'd never be able to take Schiller with them. Have you seen him?

RUTH. No. But I know he's here.

STILTON (*moving to the door up* C) They're not going to get away with this. I'm going to see the Officer in charge of the guard.

RUTH (*moving to Stilton*) No, Arthur, don't.

STILTON (*turning on her*) Don't! Are you mad? What do you think will happen to us if they find we've been helping to hide an escaped prisoner?

RUTH. But you don't understand, Arthur. The Captain . . .

STILTON (*interrupting; angrily*) I understand only too well. This Reverend Mother is trying to make damned fools of us. Do you think they'll believe we didn't know Schiller was in the Mission? These Missionaries are trouble enough when they're our own people. You don't think I'm going to stick my neck out for some bloody German priest, do you?

RUTH (*crossing below the table*) It's not that . . .

STILTON. What's the matter with you, Ruth? Have you forgotten what they did to our own son—a kid of eighteen? Did Schiller's people give him a chance when he tried to escape? Damn Schiller, let him have a taste of his own medicine.

RUTH. That's how I felt, Arthur—but Captain Lee makes a difference.

STILTON (*moving* LC) Who the hell is Captain Lee?

RUTH. The officer in charge of those soldiers. He's an Englishman of sorts.

STILTON. An Englishman? What the devil is he doing with Mei Cheng's army?

RUTH. It seems to have had something to do with his not going to Eton.

STILTON. Don't be stupid. Who is he?

RUTH. He's . . .

(LEE *enters up* C)

Speak of the Devil. (*To Lee*) Have you come to make another search—or just knock a few nuns about?

LEE. Shut up!

STILTON. Here, take it easy.

LEE. Good morning, Stilton. Tell your wife to watch her tongue—it might get her into trouble.

STILTON. That's some advice you might take yourself. Who the devil are you? How do you know me?

LEE. A sergeant examined your papers at the gate, didn't he? I've come to see what you want.

STILTON. I've come to see my wife, if it's any of your business.

LEE. Everything that goes on around here is my business. Is that the only reason?

STILTON. Why else should I come here?

Scene 2 A LETTER FROM THE GENERAL

LEE. I wondered if you had any news from the Capital. Have you been there?

STILTON. Yes. And I have a visa and exit permits for the five nuns, my wife and myself. We leave on the steamer tomorrow with General Mei Cheng's permission. I'll show them to you—tomorrow.

LEE. Hear whether they caught that Jerry priest?

STILTON. The authorities aren't likely to discuss German Nationals with me. I'm the British Consul.

LEE. Fair enough. (*He moves below the table. Casually*) I've got an idea he might be around somewhere. "Schiller" is his name. If you see him, I want him—get it? Or you might as well tear up that visa.

STILTON. How do you come to be wearing that uniform?

LEE (*moving to* L *of the table*) I put it on when I got dressed this morning. (*He puts his foot up on the chair* L *of the table*)

RUTH. It was all on account of him leaving school at fourteen.

LEE. I told you to shut up.

STILTON (*tensely*) I should advise you to watch your language, Lee—or you may find yourself flat on your back.

LEE. Then you'll find yourself in clink. The People's Republican Army don't like their officers knocked flat on their backs. (*He moves menacingly to Stilton*) Not that you'd be able to do it.

(STILTON *looks as though he is going to hit Lee*)

RUTH. Arthur—don't be a fool. He'd like nothing better.

LEE (*smiling mirthlessly*) She's right, Arthur. There's nothing I'd enjoy more than a poke at one of your sort.

(STILTON *drops his hand.* LEE *moves* RC.
  MAGDALEN *enters* L)

MAGDALEN (*peering at them*) Sister Henry says the Consul is wanting to see me.

STILTON (*moving to* R *of Magdalen*) Are you Sister Magdalen? (*He takes a letter from his pocket*)

MAGDALEN. I am.

STILTON (*holding out the letter*) I have a letter for you.

(LEE *moves quickly between Stilton and Magdalen and snatches the letter*)

LEE. I'll take that. (*He is about to open the letter*)

STILTON. Look at the seal before you open that letter.

LEE (*looking at the seal*) Mei Cheng!

MAGDALEN. Oh! A letter from the General—for me? (*Her face breaks into a smile of happiness*)

LEE (*handing the letter to Magdalen*) So it seems. You'd better open it.

MAGDALEN. I'd as soon read it in my room. I'm the General's godmother, do you see.

LEE. You don't mean to tell me that bandit has a godmother!
MAGDALEN. Peter was a fine lad. Sure, I know he's with some dreadful people. But he'd only be there for any bit of good he can do.
LEE. "Peter"? Is that what you call him?
MAGDALEN. And why wouldn't I? Isn't it his Christian name?
LEE. I should think he ought to have a Christian name. Why didn't you call him "Nero"? He was the fellow who used to throw the Christians to the lions, wasn't he?
MAGDALEN. What are you saying?
LEE. From what I know of Mei Cheng the only time he goes to Sunday School now is when he wants to burn it down.

(MAGDALEN *looks distressed.* RUTH *crosses to her*)

RUTH (*to Lee*) Why can't you keep your mouth shut? What sort of a man are you?
LEE. Get your wife out of here, Stilton, if you want her to go on that steamer in one piece. She's getting on my nerves.
STILTON. Not as much as you're getting on mine.
MAGDALEN (*to Lee*) What are you doing yourself with the Communists, and you an Englishman? I don't believe Peter would know he had the like of yourself under him in his army—I shall write to him about you. (*She moves* L)
LEE. He not only knows—he sent me here. After one of your priests—Father Schiller. Know him?
MAGDALEN. Indeed I do. He's often at the Mission with us.
LEE (*keenly*) Is he here now?
MAGDALEN. He is not. Sure, we've been worried about him. (*She moves to* L *of Lee*) He's not said Holy Mass here a month since. What would the like of yourself want with him?
LEE. I've just told you, I've come after him—to arrest him. Your godson wants him back in prison—he had him there but he escaped.
MAGDALEN. I don't believe you.
LEE (*vindictively*) Don't you? Ask your Reverend Mother—she's got a damned good idea where Schiller is. He must find it difficult to get about—General Mei Cheng had him hanging by his feet. It's one of your godson's favourite ways of getting co-operation from his prisoners.
STILTON. For God's sake, man . . .
LEE. Shut up!
MAGDALEN (*bewildered*) That—that's not true.
LEE. Isn't it? When you see Father Schiller again—*if* you see him again, get him to show you his ankles. Peter uses nasty rough ropes for his tricks. Did you teach him that one at Sunday School?
MAGDALEN (*looking at Ruth and Stilton*) It's not true—is it?
RUTH (*embarrassed*) I don't know. (*She turns away* L)
MAGDALEN. He'd never do that to Father Schiller. He couldn't

Scene 2   A LETTER FROM THE GENERAL

—not Peter. Sure, he'd spend hours with a poor bird that was injured. He wouldn't—Peter. (*She looks beseechingly at them all*)

(LEE *stands smiling coldly.* STILTON *and* RUTH *look at the floor.*
MAGDALEN *turns and exits slowly* L, *the letter in her hand and tears streaming down her face. There is a silence*)

STILTON. Come and help me get my things out of the car, Ruth.

(STILTON *and* RUTH, *studiously ignoring Lee, exit up* C. LEE *is quite unperturbed as he watches them go. He takes out his flask, crosses and flops into the armchair and takes a swig.*
The REVEREND MOTHER *enters down* L *and crosses to* C)

LEE (*without rising*) Good morning.
REV. MOTHER. Good morning to you, Captain Lee. What can we do for you?
LEE. You can tell me where Schiller is?
REV. MOTHER. Your search didn't satisfy you?
LEE. No—but I can wait. If he's here you can't take him on the steamer with you—and you're going tomorrow whether you like it or not.
REV. MOTHER. Would you answer a question for me?
LEE. I'll try. I'd like to show you that a straightforward question can get a straightforward answer.
REV. MOTHER. Sister Bridget says the Ling family are gone.
LEE. The what family?
REV. MOTHER. The native family living in the hut in our grounds.
LEE. Oh, yes—they've gone all right.
REV. MOTHER. Would you tell me where they've gone?
LEE. Don't ask me.
REV. MOTHER. Aren't your soldiers checking everyone who passes in and out of the Mission? Do you mean to tell me you've no knowledge of their disappearance?
LEE (*thoughtfully*) I wouldn't say that.
REV. MOTHER. I'd be glad to hear this straightforward answer you were going to give me.
LEE. It was this way. I was lying in my tent last night—when suddenly that hut came into my mind.
REV. MOTHER. Yes?
LEE. It was a bit nippy in the tent—and the more I thought about that hut the better I liked it. Suit me down to the ground.
REV. MOTHER (*crossing to* L *of Lee; coldly*) Are you telling me that you turned those poor creatures out in the middle of the night—and took the hut for yourself?
LEE. That's right.
REV. MOTHER. Then it was a foolish thing you did.
LEE (*rising angrily*) You think so? Then let me tell you you're damned lucky I haven't taken over the whole Mission and billeted my men here.

(Ruth *and* Stilton *enter up* c, *carrying three suitcases*)

Stilton (*crossing down* l) Throwing your weight about again, Lee? (*He puts his cases on the floor*) You do pick on women, don't you?

(Ruth *moves down* l *and puts her case on the floor*)

Lee (*crossing to Stilton*) I'll pick on you any time you like.

Rev. Mother. I'm still waiting to hear where the Ling family would be.

Lee (*crossing to* l *of the Reverend Mother*) The last I saw of them they were running like rabbits in the dark with my men firing over their heads. The old man had too much lip—but don't worry yourself, these natives can look after themselves better than you can.

Rev. Mother. The Ling family were in our care—you hadn't the right to treat them that way.

Lee (*harshly*) Understand this. I represent the Government and I've a right to treat them any way I like. You can squeak to the Consul here about what I do to you, but Schiller and the Lings are my meat. (*Smoothly*) As a matter of fact I was pretty decent. I slung a lot of their stuff after them—except the old man's bed. That was a bit of all right—a damned sight better than my sleeping bag. Best night's sleep I've had for months.

Rev. Mother. Didn't you notice anything about them—the Lings, I mean?

Lee (*impatiently*) Oh, forget them. They're all right. The old man got a few kicks for his cheek—that won't hurt him—it's all these people understand.

Ruth. It must have made a nice change for you—knocking old men about.

Lee. I thought you'd have to stick your oar in—shut *up*. (*To the Reverend Mother*) Now you know it all—I've taken that hut over as my personal headquarters.

Rev. Mother. I see.

Lee. We'll have no more talk about it. (*He moves to the door up* c *and turns*) I shall be more comfortable there. Smell of joss-sticks or something, but that'll wear off.

Rev. Mother. You've not been in the country a great while, have you, Captain Lee? That smell isn't joss-sticks at all—ask your men what it is—they'll tell you.

Lee (*moving to* l *of the Reverend Mother*) What do you mean?

Rev. Mother. You seem to have everything under control, Captain—I'd not like to spoil your illusions.

Lee. Oh, come off it. I suppose you're going to tell me that the old man's ancestors will come back and haunt me. He's put an Oriental curse on me.

Rev. Mother (*moving down* r) By sleeping in that bed you might well have incurred one of the oldest curses of the Orient.

Scene 2   A LETTER FROM THE GENERAL   43

LEE (*moving* RC; *roughly*) What are you talking about?

REV. MOTHER (*calmly*) Ling Hu and his family are lepers.

(LEE *looks incredulously at the Reverend Mother. He seems to shrivel physically. His mouth hangs open and he clutches the chair* L *of the table. There is a silence as the others stare at Lee*)

LEE (*hissing*) Leprosy!

REV. MOTHER. I'm afraid so.

LEE (*panic welling up in him*) Why wasn't I told . . .?

REV. MOTHER. I never thought you'd take it on yourself to trouble a poor afflicted family like the Lings. Even so, I'd have thought you'd have sense enough to see the sickness that was on them.

LEE. But—but—why didn't they say . . .?

REV. MOTHER. They were too busy dodging kicks and bullets.

LEE. Lepers! That bed! (*He collapses on to the chair* L *of the table. In the last few moments he has become almost a wreck*)

REV. MOTHER. I'd say you were unduly distressed, Captain Lee. You've done a foolish thing but it's not likely you've contracted leprosy. I've attended lepers for twenty years on and off, and never a sign of infection.

RUTH. I don't suppose you slept in their beds.

REV. MOTHER. I've taken precautions, naturally. One or two missionaries have been infected—but it's a thing that seldom happens.

RUTH (*eyeing Lee; vindictively*) I don't think it would be fair to raise the Captain's hopes. Personally, I can't think of a more fitting reward for him.

LEE (*rising; wildly*) I've got to get away from here. (*He crosses to Stilton*) You must get me to a doctor. Get me away.

STILTON. Get you away? Are you insane? (*Ironically*) Aren't there any doctors in the People's Republican Army?

LEE. You don't understand. They won't bother with me if I've got leprosy. They don't have any truck with lepers, more often than not they just leave them to die. (*Almost in tears*) Especially me, I'm not one of them. I'm English, you're the British Consul, you must help me—I want an English doctor.

(STILTON, *unmoved, watches Lee*)

(*He looks from one to the other, then crosses to Ruth and appeals to her*) You're his wife, you could make him take me on the boat—I could say I was going on as a guard or something. You can't leave me here—with this hanging over me.

RUTH (*enjoying herself*) I don't see why not. You'll be useful to the People's Republican Army for a few years yet. You can still fire a gun, until you lose your limbs, but that's at the later stages . . .

(*The* REVEREND MOTHER, *seeing the terror on* LEE'S *face, interrupts and crosses to Lee*)

Rev. Mother. That's enough, Mrs Stilton. (*She leads Lee to the armchair*) Captain Lee, I apologize for the alarm I'm causing you.

(Lee *collapses into the armchair*)

I'd like you to know that I was not being vindictive. I had the duty to warn you of the risk you had run, even such a slight one.

(Lee *buries his face in his hands*)

It would be safer to take precautions in any case.

Lee (*clutching at her habit*) Precautions? What precautions? What can I do?

Ruth. You can throw yourself in the Yellow River for my part. (*She picks up her case*) Come on, Arthur.

(Ruth *casts a derisive look at Lee and exits* L
Stilton *picks up his cases and follows* Ruth *off*)

Lee (*still clutching the Reverend Mother's habit*) How soon would I know? How soon would I know whether . . .? (*He stops and looks up at her*)

Rev. Mother (*calmly*) The symptoms might not show for two or three years.

Lee (*in a panic*) Two or three years! I couldn't stand it—I'd rather shoot myself. I will—I'll . . .

Rev. Mother (*sharply*) Have sense, man. I was going to tell you what can be done for you to set your mind at rest. Doctors can't diagnose it straight off—but they can give injections as a precaution. We treat leprosy with oils, but I'm told there is a more up-to-date treatment with sulphur drugs.

Lee (*eagerly*) That's what I want—I want a doctor. Couldn't you get one of your Missionary doctors to give me some treatment? Get one to come here.

Rev. Mother (*moving* C; *impatiently*) That would prove nothing to you. There's small chance you've contracted the disease, anyway. You're making a great palaver about nothing.

Lee. Nothing, you call it! It's all right for you to say that, you've got nothing to worry about. I don't want to live for years watching the flesh rot off my own body. I've seen 'em about, they frighten me. (*He shouts*) Only a slight chance! I don't want *no* chance! Do you understand? I don't want a million to one chance.

Rev. Mother. And how would I find a doctor for you? (*She turns on Lee almost viciously*) Do you know who was our doctor? Father Schiller!

Lee. Schiller! The Jerry!

Rev. Mother. He was. The man you've had tortured and beaten. The man you're hunting now to take back to torture and death.

Lee (*rising; eagerly*) You're wrong. I wouldn't turn him in— not now. (*He moves to her*) You can get him for me—you must.

(*The* Reverend Mother *looks expressionlessly at Lee*)

Scene 2   A LETTER FROM THE GENERAL   45

Rev. Mother (*after a pause*) I'd be a foolish woman to trust you, Captain Lee, even if I could find Father Schiller.

Lee. You can find him—you must have seen him or how would you know they'd tortured and beaten him?

Rev. Mother. Isn't it the usual treatment for religious prisoners? I'd as soon sign Father Schiller's death warrant as bring him to you.

Lee. That would be all right. Look, I'm certain you've got him here somewhere. I'll show you, I won't do a thing about it —if I wanted to I could have the men in and get him, couldn't I?

Rev. Mother. I happen to know your orders don't permit you to bring your men in on us unless you're sure Father Schiller is with us—and you aren't sure.

(Lee *kneels to the Reverend Mother*)

Lee (*pleading*) Just ask him to see me. You could get a message to him—I know you could, even if he's not here now. If you've got him away he can't be far. (*He is almost in tears*) Please.

Rev. Mother. Captain Lee. I'll see if a message can be given to Father Schiller—it shall be his decision. (*She moves to the door up* c) Meantime, search for the Ling family. Remember, what is happening to Ling Hu now, could be happening to you in a few years' time.

The Reverend Mother *exits up* c. Lee *rises, takes out his flask and drinks, then lurches despairingly out up* c *as—*

the Curtain *falls*

ACT III

SCENE—*The same. The evening of the same day.*

When the CURTAIN *rises, the bookcases are empty and the desk and table are cleared. Only the furniture, lamps and crucifix remain. Obviously everything is packed ready to leave. The armchair* R *is now* LC. *The lamp* R *is lit.* BRIDGET *is at the table, packing a few remaining books into a box.* LUCY *enters up* C.

LUCY. They've robbed us of twelve of them chickens.

BRIDGET. Ah, sure, we'd never be takin' the chickens with us at all.

LUCY. After the trouble they've brought on us all they don't deserve to be eating our chickens.

BRIDGET. Have charity, Sister Lucy. (*She smiles*) At least we've not seen himself all day.

LUCY. The Captain, do you mean? Good riddance to the man. I expect he's out there all the same. I'm wondering if he found the Ling family.

BRIDGET. According to the Consul's wife, he's thinking only of himself. She says he was almost crying and slobbering on the floor when he heard where he was after sleeping.

LUCY. Small blame to the man for that. I've always had a fear of leprosy myself. But then, you could worry yourself skinny and maybe you'd never catch it.

BRIDGET. I looked in the cupboard, there's not a thing worth taking there.

LUCY. I'm right sick of that cupboard. We'll forget it—unless Reverend Mother brings it to mind. What I'm worried about is Father Schiller. We can't leave the poor man here.

BRIDGET. Ah, sure, we'll think of something.

LUCY. You always say that, and supposing we don't? What if the Captain comes for him with the soldiers? The second we've gone he'll be in here.

(*The* REVEREND MOTHER *enters* L, *crosses to* C *and looks around*)

REV. MOTHER. Have you finished, Sisters?

BRIDGET. I think this is the last box, Reverend Mother.

REV. MOTHER (*looking at the cupboard*) What about that cupboard? Have you been through it to see if there's anything we'd be needing?

(LUCY *and* BRIDGET *look at each other*)

BRIDGET. Well, I was saying, Reverend Mother, there's a terrible lot of junk in there.

REV. MOTHER (*smiling*) And a terrible lot of work to clear it out?

BRIDGET. Well, there is that, too.

Rev. Mother. Leave it, then. We'll most likely have to leave half we've packed already. (*She sits wearily above the table*)

Lucy. They've had twelve of the chickens, Reverend Mother.

Rev. Mother. It's probably the first decent meal the poor soldiers have had in months. You can hardly blame them.

Bridget. I'd sooner we'd eaten them ourselves. Reverend Mother—Mrs Stilton says Sister Magdalen had a letter from the General this morning, brought by the Consul. Have you seen the letter?

Rev. Mother. It was a personal letter. Sister Magdalen said nothing about it to me. I'm sure she'll have the goodness to show me if there's anything I ought to know.

Bridget. I didn't mean to be nosey, Reverend Mother—but you know how it is—any bit of news . . .

Rev. Mother. I know, child.

Lucy. Is it worried about Father Schiller you are, Reverend Mother?

Rev. Mother. I am. There seems very little hope for him.

Bridget. You'd never think so to speak with him—him saying Mass this morning and hardly able to stand.

Rev. Mother. If only he could be put on the steamer. (*She sighs*) I see no way of doing it. Did the Consul come back yet?

Lucy. I've not seen him. Why did he go to the Capital?

Rev. Mother. He had business there.

(Henry *enters* L *and crosses to* C. *She appears angry*)

Henry. I don't understand that woman. If you're decent to her she'll make some smart remark—then you'll answer her back and she's sweet as sugar.

Rev. Mother. If it's Mrs Stilton you mean, she's an unhappy soul. I'd say her life has been empty since she lost her son. Her husband is no great help to her, either.

Lucy. She's not given us away yet. Did she tell her husband about Father Schiller?

Henry (*moving up* L) I don't know—but I shouldn't think he's any greater love for the Germans than she has herself. (*She lights the lamp up* L)

(Magdalen *enters down* L. *She looks very bright and cheerful*)

Magdalen. Reverend Mother, I'm just after talking to Father Schiller. Why didn't you tell me he was here, and him saying Mass this morning?

Rev. Mother. I didn't want to worry you, Sister Magdalen. What did Father Schiller say to you?

Magdalen. Sure, I only spoke to him for a minute. He was at his Office. They want to capture him again, don't they?

Rev. Mother. I'm afraid so.

Magdalen (*thoughtfully*) If he could make away with us—on the steamer.

Rev. Mother. I've been thinking on that, Sister Magdalen. There's no way at all. We only have exit permits for the five of us.
Magdalen. I think I know a way it can be done.
Rev. Mother. How?
Magdalen. I had a letter from Peter. Did you know?
Rev. Mother. I heard there was a letter. Does he mention Father Schiller?
Magdalen. No—but he's asking me to stay.
Rev. Mother (*rising; aghast*) The General wants you to stay here?
Magdalen. Not here—at the Capital. He's after asking me to go there and take charge of a home he's opening for our orphans. Until the Government can take charge of it.
Rev. Mother. But, Sister Magdalen—you couldn't do a thing like that. You'd expect us to leave you here—alone? No, I'll not give a second's thought to the idea.
Magdalen. I'd a hope you might give me permission to stay.
Rev. Mother. I will not. In any case, how would that help Father Schiller?
Magdalen (*eagerly*) Sure, he could go on the steamer in place of me.
Henry (*moving down* L) I don't set the intelligence of the soldiers at a great height—but even they could see that Father Schiller wasn't Sister Magdalen.
Magdalen. Not if he wore one of our habits.
Rev. Mother. You mean, to dress Father Schiller up like a nun?
Magdalen. And why not? They don't know me—except that Captain. He was here when the Consul gave me Peter's letter.
Rev. Mother. Do you have the letter with you?
Magdalen. Peter asked me to destroy it; he said it was best.
Rev. Mother. He did . . . (*She pauses*) No, I wouldn't countenance such a scheme. Nor would Father Schiller.
Magdalen (*crossing to* L *of the Reverend Mother; sadly*) Reverend Mother—wouldn't you let me stay here—with my children? (*Brokenly*) They've been my life, the children of this country. I—I—know well enough I should go back with you, but you are all young enough, even yourself, to make a fresh beginning. I could never put my heart into another life. My heart is here in this country. I've spent my life trying to bring a knowledge of God to the poor orphans and I want to finish my life among them. (*Strongly*) And what'll become of me if I go back to Ireland? I'll never be sent on the Missions again—I'll be like some old horse put out in a field. I'll be sitting in some Home with a lot of old nuns—and I'll sit all the day thinking of my children here; the heat and the sweat on me after a day's work will be a memory. (*Pleadingly*) Don't let me leave to die like that. I've not long to live—let me spend me last few years with me children. (*She turns away, sobbing*)

(*There is a silence as the others look from Magdalen to the Reverend Mother*)

Rev. Mother. Sit down, Sister Magdalen. (*She sits Magdalen in the chair* L *of the table*) I can't think what I should say to you. If I let you stay what do you think they'd do to you when they found Father Schiller was gone on the steamer with us? They'd put the blame on you—then ... (*She makes a despairing gesture with her hands*)

Magdalen. I've thought about that.

Rev. Mother. Then you'll see your idea is impossible.

Magdalen. But you would have left Father Schiller. Why not me? I know I'd not be able to do a lot for the children by myself —but I'd do something. And Peter won't be hard on me—not when I tell him the way of things.

Henry. I wouldn't be too sure about that. He had Father Schiller arrested.

Magdalen. He had orders to do so. Even a General has to obey his superiors. (*To the Reverend Mother*) This is the one and only time in my religious life I've ever asked anything for myself. And think to the work Father Schiller would do if he was to escape. He's another twenty years in the service of God. A fine missionary and a doctor, too.

Henry (*moving* c) And what about Captain Lee? Would he be sitting watching Father Schiller walking on the steamer dressed as a nun?

Rev. Mother. I'm not worried about Captain Lee.

Henry. And why not, in the name of God?

Rev. Mother (*moving to* R *of Henry*) Captain Lee is terrified he may have contracted leprosy. He's promised not to arrest Father Schiller if he can see him and get medical attention.

Henry. Do you mean you'd trust a bargain with Captain Lee? The man would sell his own soul.

Rev. Mother. Every man can be trusted, Sister Henry—at times.

Lucy. But what would Father Schiller do for him? He couldn't tell now if the man had leprosy.

Rev. Mother. It's a matter of psychology. The possibility may be remote but it preys on the mind. A few words and an injection from Father Schiller would go far to set Captain Lee's mind at rest.

Henry. The whole idea is ridiculous. The man doesn't deserve a minute's consideration. If he had leprosy it would be no more than he deserved—a just punishment from God Himself.

Rev. Mother. I think it's always better to let God give His own punishments than arrange them for Him, Sister Henry.

(Henry *turns away down* L)

Magdalen. Would you let me stay, then, Reverend Mother?

Rev. Mother. I—I—don't know. You put me in an awkward position, Sister Magdalen. As your Superior I should say "no"—but as your friend . . .

Magdalen. If the Captain would let Father Schiller on the steamer—then could I be staying here?

(*The* Reverend Mother *does not reply. She paces up* c)

(*She follows up her advantage*) If I tell you myself that I won't go with the steamer—(*she rises*) will it relieve you of the load of responsibility?

Rev. Mother (*turning slowly and facing Magdalen*) I've spent many years in this country with you, Magdalen—and far from feeling your Superior, I've always looked to you as an example. I know your feelings, and I know how strong they must be for you to talk of breaking your vow of Obedience. (*She moves to* L *of Magdalen*) If the Captain agrees to Father Schiller going in your place you may stay—with my permission. (*Her voice breaks*) And may God forgive me if I am wrong.

Magdalen. Thank you, Reverend Mother. And have no fear; it's the right thing you're doing. I think I'll away to my room, now, Reverend Mother, just for a while. It's tired I am.

(Magdalen *crosses and exits* L)

Henry. But what about Father Schiller?

Rev. Mother. I shall tell him that Sister Magdalen has been asked to stay by General Mei Cheng and she has my permission.

Bridget. You can be sure that Captain Lee won't be telling General Mei Cheng that he has let Father Schiller escape, so they won't take it out on Sister Magdalen.

Rev. Mother (*suddenly brisk*) Is everything ready for our journey, Sisters?

Bridget. It is, Reverend Mother.

Lucy. I wish there was some way of taking the chickens.

Bridget. If we could eat about four each for supper, that'd get them out of the way. Oh, I forgot me Agatha Christies! (*She crosses to the door* L) I wonder if they'd get past the Customs here—all that violence?

Rev. Mother. Would yourself and Sister Lucy make certain there's no vestments left in the Chapel?

Lucy. Sure, Reverend Mother. Come along, Bridget—your silly murder books can wait.

(Lucy *and* Bridget *exit* L)

Rev. Mother (*looking at Henry*) Well, Sister Henry, I suppose you will want to offer me advice.

Henry. No, Reverend Mother—I shall pray for you.

Rev. Mother. I'd sooner you did that. I've made my decision.

(Schiller *enters* L. *He walks unsteadily.* Henry *goes to* Schiller *and leads him to the armchair* LC)

ACT III   A LETTER FROM THE GENERAL

HENRY. Sit yourself here, Father. Are you feeling better?
SCHILLER (*sitting in the armchair* LC) Well enough, child.
HENRY (*moving up* C *and closing the shutters*) I think these will be better closed. I have no great trust in Captain Lee's reformation.

(*The* REVEREND MOTHER *crosses to* R *of Schiller*)

SCHILLER. Ja! This man who wishes to see a doctor?
HENRY. A most unpleasant fellow he is.
SCHILLER. Hm! An Englishman who fights with the Communists. What can I do for him, though? (*He raises his hands in a gesture of bewilderment*) He sleeps in a leper's bed, so—does that mean he has taken the disease? I tell you it is not easy for Europeans to contract this thing. Perhaps, yes—but most unlikely.
REV. MOTHER. It's more a question of the way the man feels himself, Father. He is terrified and if you see him, he has promised to let you escape.
SCHILLER. You mean, I should leave on the steamer with you? But how? Will not the Captain check the exit permits?
REV. MOTHER. Sister Magdalen wants to stay here. With the Captain's help we could use her permit for you, Father. That is —if you wear one of her habits.
SCHILLER. You mean that I should dress like a nun? (*He smiles*) But Sister Magdalen—you say she will stay here?
REV. MOTHER. General Mei Cheng is her godson—she brought him up as a child. He wishes her to stay and found a State Orphanage. She might well do a lot of good by staying.
SCHILLER. That is true. But if I am discovered on the boat it will be bad for you.
REV. MOTHER. You will not be discovered. Our first call is a British port on the Island of Yakmu. The only problem is the exit permit—which we have.
SCHILLER. I do not care for this plan.
REV. MOTHER. We've given it great thought, Father. As Superior I take responsibility.

(*There is a knock at the door up* C. HENRY *looks through the shutter*)

HENRY. It's the Consul.
REV. MOTHER. Let him in.
SCHILLER. He knows I'm here?
REV. MOTHER. His wife may well have told him.

(HENRY *unbolts the door up* C.
STILTON *enters up* C. *He is obviously pleased with himself*)

STILTON. Hello, all bolted and barred? (*He sees Schiller and his attitude changes immediately*) Oh . . .
REV. MOTHER. This is Father Schiller, Mr Stilton.
STILTON (*coldly*) Good evening.
SCHILLER. Excuse me, please, for not rising—my ankles . . .

STILTON. I heard you had trouble with them.
REV. MOTHER. Did you have a successful trip to the Capital, Mr Stilton?
STILTON (*moving to* L *of the table*) Very. Can you leave here this evening? (*He perches on the table*)
REV. MOTHER. Tonight?
STILTON. As soon as you are ready.
HENRY. But the steamer isn't due till tomorrow at the very earliest.
STILTON. It won't be here for a week.
REV. MOTHER. Then how . . .?
STILTON. We're going to fly from Mukin airfield.
HENRY. Fly?
STILTON. Yes. The steamer is laid up for a few days—repairs. So I took a chance and raised Cain. Got in to see Mei Cheng and he's chartered a plane for us tonight. Only one of their old carrier crates—probably have to sit on the floor—but we should be eating a civilized breakfast tomorrow.
REV. MOTHER. But our belongings—there'll be little enough room for ourselves.
STILTON. Mei Cheng says he'll arrange to have your stuff sent on the steamer.
HENRY. I wonder.
STILTON. Well, he doesn't say a great deal to me, but I have the impression that as far as you people are concerned it's now or never. I've got my station wagon here—seven of us can pack in there at a pinch.

(RUTH *enters* L)

RUTH (*crossing to Stilton*) Oh, hello—you're back . . . (*She sees Schiller and stops* C)
SCHILLER. I have to thank you for not betraying me last night.
RUTH. Don't mention it. My dislike of Captain Lee outweighed my dislike of Germans at that particular moment. (*She turns her back on Schiller and faces Stilton*)
STILTON. We're getting out by plane—tonight, Ruth.
RUTH. Good God! How did you manage that?
STILTON. Never mind—it's arranged. (*He rises and moves down* R)
RUTH. All of us?
STILTON (*with a look at Schiller*) Yes—the five Sisters and we two.
REV. MOTHER. Sister Magdalen is staying.
STILTON. Staying? But I've got an exit permit for her.
REV. MOTHER. She's had the offer of a post from the General if she stays. 'Twas the letter you brought yourself this morning.
STILTON. You mean she *wants* to remain here?
REV. MOTHER. I do. She's going to be here to care for our orphan children for a while.

Act III   A LETTER FROM THE GENERAL   53

STILTON. She must be mad. Then we shall have to send back her exit permit.

REV. MOTHER. No. We want to use it for Father Schiller—he can wear a nun's habit.

STILTON. Do you want us all shot?

SCHILLER. I think you are right to protest, Herr Stilton. I assure you this is the idea of the Reverend Mother.

RUTH. What about Lee? Do you think you can pass Schiller off on him as a nun?

REV. MOTHER. I may be able to arrange matters with Captain Lee.

RUTH (*turning to Schiller*) I'd like to see you try. I'm not risking my neck for any bloody German.

SCHILLER (*rising painfully*) Mrs Stilton, please, I do not wish you to take any risk for me.

RUTH. We aren't going to—don't worry. Your people have already murdered my son.

SCHILLER. Many people were killed in the war, Mrs Stilton—on both sides. Nevertheless, I appreciate your feelings—I would only point out to you that there are good and bad Germans as there are of any nationality. We are all human beings.

STILTON. I don't want to listen to any sermons, Schiller. I simply want to make it clear that you aren't going to be responsible for my death and my wife's. (*He moves to* R *of Ruth*)

(*The* REVEREND MOTHER *motions to Schiller to sit.* SCHILLER *resumes his seat*)

REV. MOTHER. Mr Stilton—the risk would be negligible if the Captain agrees—the pilot of the aeroplane won't know Sister Magdalen.

RUTH. And what makes you think Lee will agree?

REV. MOTHER. Didn't you hear the man raving? He wants to see a doctor—Father Schiller is a doctor . . .

RUTH. You don't mean to say Schiller is going to see Captain Lee? (*She looks incredulously at Schiller*) He might just as well shoot himself.

SCHILLER. If the man needs me—I must see him. I must take the risk.

RUTH. You were hiding in that trunk—you heard what he was like. How do you think he can be trusted?

SCHILLER. Is it my place to ask if he can be trusted? He asks for help—he is sick in his body. I shall do what I can for him—the more so for he is sick in his soul.

STILTON. That's your affair. But to my mind you'd do better to lie low until we are gone—then make a break for it. It's your best plan.

SCHILLER. My best plan perhaps—but not my duty. It may be that God has permitted me to escape—to help this one man.

(LEE, *off, is heard drunkenly singing "Roll Out the Barrel". They all listen*)

HENRY. It's Captain Lee. (*She rushes to the door*)
SCHILLER (*authoritatively*) Sister—leave the door, please.

(*They all eye the door apprehensively with glances at* SCHILLER *who remains quite calm in his chair. The singing stops.*
LEE *enters up* C. *He stands there, dishevelled and drunk. The others stare silently at him. He glares round the room and sees Schiller*)

LEE (*moving* C) You—you've got him for me.
REV. MOTHER. Father Schiller is here if you're wanting him.
LEE (*moving to* R *of Schiller*) Of course I want him. Did they tell you what I'd done? Did they tell you I slept in that stinking bed last night? You've got to do something for me. D'you hear?
SCHILLER. I shall do what I can—which is very little.
LEE. You've got something you can give me, haven't you? You're always treating lepers. I don't care what I have to do. I'm not afraid of pain. I'm not afraid of anything except this. You've got to help me.
REV. MOTHER. Captain Lee. We shall be leaving here within an hour or so.
LEE (*sharply*) Leaving? Don't pull that—the earliest that boat can be here is tomorrow.
STILTON. The Reverend Mother is correct. I have the exit permits and we leave from Mukin airfield tonight.
LEE. That's all right—but he's not leaving. Not Schiller.
REV. MOTHER (*moving to* R *of Lee*) That's what I'd like to talk to you about, Captain. General Mei Cheng has asked Sister Magdalen to stay—we want to take Father Schiller in her place.
LEE. How can you do that?
REV. MOTHER. We should let him wear a nun's habit—he can use Sister Magdalen's exit permit.
LEE. Smart, eh?
REV. MOTHER. You'd have to co-operate with us. If your men escort us to the airfield—the pilot will accept him as Sister Magdalen. Do you see that?
LEE. You want me to help him escape? Christ! I'd be shot!
REV. MOTHER. It need never be known that he had escaped— or anyway, that it was your fault. Father Schiller has offered to help you—and you've given your word you'd not arrest him.
LEE. You are smart. (*He looks at Schiller, then back at the Reverend Mother*) I don't have much option, do I? But what about me? (*He suddenly looks at Schiller*) You've got to do something for me, Schiller, do you hear? (*His voice has a ring of terror*) There must be something you can do—I've had this hanging over me all day —I've been drinking—but I can't forget it.
RUTH (*to Stilton*) I'm going to pack. (*She crosses to* R *of Lee*) I'm terribly worried about you, Captain. When I get back to Eng-

land, I'm going to send you a little bell, with your name inscribed on it.

LEE (*stupidly*) A bell . . .?

RUTH. Yes. I understand you have to wear one and call "unclean". You could have done that before you slept in the bed . . .

LEE (*grasping Ruth's arm*) Why you—cow!

STILTON (*rushing at Lee*) How dare you!

(LEE *turns to Stilton and knocks him down.* STILTON *rises and* LEE *is about to hit him again*)

SCHILLER (*rising; his voice ringing out compellingly*) Captain Lee!

(LEE *stops.*

RUTH, *unperturbed, crosses and exits* L.

STILTON, *with a look of hatred at Lee, follows her off*)

(*He moves the chair* L *of the table to* C. *To Lee*) Sit down.

(LEE *sits wearily* C. *All the fight has gone out of him. He buries his face in his hands*)

Sister Henry, bring me my bag, please. The one from that cupboard in my room.

HENRY. Mrs Stilton will be there—oh, what does that matter?

(HENRY *exits* L)

SCHILLER (*to Lee*) You understand that I can do no more for you than the Sister could have done. You asked for me—so, I will treat you.

LEE (*weakly*) I'll do anything—anything you say.

SCHILLER. All I can do is inject with Chaulmoogra Oil. It is the standard treatment for those infected with leprosy. You cannot know whether you have contracted the disease for months—even years. These injections will arrest the disease if not cure.

REV. MOTHER. Infection wouldn't be likely, would it now, Father?

SCHILLER (*shrugging*) Perhaps no—but if one is to get this thing it can come from sleeping in an infected bed—as a doctor I must say this. As a priest I would tell you I have known lepers for many years who lived lives full of happiness—their souls were at peace and . . .

LEE (*interrupting*) Skip the sermon and get on with the injection, will you?

SCHILLER. The state of your soul is more important than the state of your body.

LEE. Listen! If those bastards find I've got this I won't have no body—they'll kick me out and shoot me.

(HENRY *enters* L, *carrying a black case.* SCHILLER *takes the case, puts it on the table and opens it*)

HENRY. Father, we had some of the oil for the Ling family. We found ourselves short.

SCHILLER. There is plenty here. (*He fills a hypodermic syringe with oil*) Remove his jacket, please.

REV. MOTHER. Surely, Father. (*She removes Lee's jacket, puts it on the armchair* LC, *then rolls up his sleeve*)

SCHILLER (*crossing to* LEE) You watch where I inject this. I shall leave you the bottle of oil for injections once weekly.

REV. MOTHER. A minute, Father. Captain Lee, before you have these injections demonstrated, you'll be kind enough to come with me and instruct the escort to take us to the airfield.

LEE. What is this? Don't you trust me?

REV. MOTHER (*dryly*) It would be easier for you to give the order now than when you've been treated.

LEE (*rising*) All right.

REV. MOTHER. We'll be leaving in Mr Stilton's station wagon.

(LEE *and the* REVEREND MOTHER *exit up* C. LEE *is heard off, calling in dialect*)

HENRY. I'd say you'll be coming with us, Father.

SCHILLER. It seems a way has been opened for my escape—I must take it. It seems my work is not finished.

(*Shouts in dialect are heard off*)

HENRY. And what do you think of Sister Magdalen, putting her life in the hands of Mei Cheng?

(*Shouts in dialect are heard off*)

SCHILLER. It is for the Reverend Mother to say. She is the Religious Superior. It is our life to obey.

(*Shouts in dialect are heard off*)

HENRY. It's surely a good thing the Captain is giving instructions out there before you attended him.

SCHILLER. I have a great pity for this man. He is alone in his fear. There can be nothing worse for a man.

(*The* REVEREND MOTHER *and* LEE *enter up* C)

LEE. Satisfied?

(*The* REVEREND MOTHER *nods*. LEE *sits on the chair* C)

SCHILLER. Now, watch. You can fill the hypodermic so.

(LEE *nods*)

Then you will inject yourself so. (*He makes the injection*)

(LEE *does not turn a hair. He sits quite still.* HENRY *swabs and rolls down Lee's sleeve*)

So. Now, if you should get symptoms—small brown discolorations of your skin—then you must increase the injections to twice weekly. If no symptoms occur, this bottle will last you for a year.

Act III A LETTER FROM THE GENERAL

(*He puts the syringe in a kidney dish and puts the dish and the bottle on the shelves up* R) From a hospital, you can obtain more oil—I will write the name for you. (*He takes a prescription pad and pencil from his bag, writes and gives the prescription to Lee*)

(LEE *pockets the prescription.*
          RUTH *enters* L)

RUTH. My husband says you must hurry. If you want to bring any personal luggage, be quick, he is waiting.

REV. MOTHER. Father Schiller is coming with us.

RUTH. The Captain has agreed?

REV. MOTHER. He has. He has ordered his soldiers to escort us to the airfield.

RUTH (*shrugging and moving up* L) If you want to risk it. I warn you—I shall know nothing of these arrangements.

HENRY. Will I be off to tell Lucy and Bridget, Reverend Mother?

REV. MOTHER. If you would. Come with me, will you, Father? We must see Sister Magdalen.

(HENRY *and the* REVEREND MOTHER *exit* L. LEE *sits silently in his chair*)

SCHILLER. I am grateful to you 'once again, Mrs Stilton. I am sure in time your bitterness will pass.

RUTH. Thank you. At least I know that some of the Germans who aren't swine are fools.

(SCHILLER *smiles at Ruth and exits* L. RUTH *looks at Lee, then wanders up* R. *She looks at the hypodermic syringe in the dish, then turns and looks in Schiller's case*)

RUTH. Takes me back to my war days in the Red Cross. (*She turns to Lee*) So you let Schiller go. I still think he was a fool to stick his chin out like that for you.

LEE (*almost to himself*) Yes. I shall be alone . . .

RUTH (*moving to* R *of Lee*) You've still got your friends in the People's Republican Army.

LEE (*louder*) Friends! I've got no friends! I've never had any friends—or family. I'm like Mei Cheng, a bloody orphan. (*More strongly*) But I don't need anyone—I'm as good as anybody. (*He rises and collects his jacket*) Do you hear? As good as anyone.

RUTH. I'm not deaf.

LEE. Alone and like it—that's me. I can take care of myself—always have done. (*He suddenly falters*) Until—until this came along. (*He shouts*) Why should it happen to me—tell me that. (*He looks at his hands*) I've got it, I know I've got it. I'll be watching for brown marks on my skin every day. What am I going to do? If they find I've got it they'll kick me out, I tell you. It'll be my lot. (*He stands looking at his arms, terrified*)

RUTH. What makes you so sure they'll kick you out?

LEE. They don't like me—they watch me. This is the first job they've given me on my own—and I've mucked it. Schiller's going to get away. (*Suddenly*) I won't muck it, why should he get away—I'll take him, so help me, I will.

RUTH. But haven't you arranged an escort for him?

LEE (*excitedly*) I'll damned soon disarrange it. Why should I be left here to take the can back for that Jerry escaping? I'll take him—then they'll know I'm all right—they'll trust me. Don't you see, they'll look after me—no matter what.

RUTH. What about your agreement with the Mother Superior?

LEE (*flinging down his jacket*) To hell with the Mother Superior! What would you do in my position?

RUTH. I should never have got myself into your position.

LEE. Still smart, eh? (*He moves towards the door up* C)

RUTH (*intercepting Lee and barring his way*) Where are you going?

LEE. Mind your business. Get out of my way.

(RUTH *does not move.* LEE *grabs her and pulls her round to* RC, *but she clings to him, struggling.*

STILTON *enters up* C)

STILTON. Ruth! (*He makes a lunge at Lee*)

(LEE *is caught off guard and* STILTON's *blow knocks him to the floor, unconscious*)

RUTH (*breathlessly*) Thank you.

STILTON. The swine!

RUTH. Help me get him into the chair.

(RUTH *and* STILTON *put Lee into the chair above the table.* RUTH *gets the hypodermic syringe, selects a bottle from Schiller's case, fills the syringe and gives Lee an injection*)

STILTON. What the blazes are you doing, Ruth?

RUTH. It's a sedative. Just to make sure our friend doesn't wake up till we get out of here. (*She replaces the bottle and syringe*)

STILTON. Why did he attack you?

RUTH. Give me a cigarette, will you?

(STILTON *gives Ruth a cigarette and lights it for her*)

Schiller treated him on condition he let him escape with the old nun's visa. He got his treatment, and then he changed his mind and was going to take Schiller in.

STILTON. You mean, you tried to stop him?

RUTH. Yes.

STILTON. But why? Don't you see what you've done?

RUTH. Yes—I've stopped him.

STILTON. You've done more than that. You've involved us both in smuggling this priest out of the country. You must be mad.

RUTH. Perhaps I am—I just acted on impulse.

Act III A LETTER FROM THE GENERAL

STILTON. I don't understand you, Ruth. Why this sudden affection for Schiller? Him of all people.

RUTH. It's not affection—say I just got tired of hating Germans—perhaps he cured me. (*She shrugs*) I don't know. To tell the truth he's the first one I ever met—and instead of some soulless swine breathing murder and destruction—I find a simple man in a dirty white smock who can hardly stand on his tortured feet.

STILTON. I don't think I shall ever understand women. Ruth . . . (*He pauses*)

RUTH. Yes?

STILTON (*brusquely*) Nothing. I'll get your bags. I'll take them out the side door, the car's out there—you can go straight out—I'll meet you.

(STILTON *goes to the door* L, *pauses as though to say something to Ruth, changes his mind and exits.* RUTH *sinks into the armchair* LC. HENRY *enters* L. *She is in full habit and carries a suitcase*)

HENRY (*crossing to* C) What's the matter with Captain Lee?

RUTH (*rising quickly and intercepting Henry*) He asked for a sleeping draught. He hasn't had any sleep lately. (*She indicates Schiller's case*) I fixed him up. Are the others coming?

HENRY. Yes.

RUTH. Glad to be going, aren't you?

HENRY. I think it's a tragedy, leaving Sister Magdalen behind us.

RUTH. She made her own choice. I suppose it's possible to become attached to this place.

HENRY. You can become attached to any place—if your work is well done there.

RUTH. The implication being that your work was not well done?

HENRY (*facing Ruth*) Mrs Stilton, I never liked you from the first minute I saw you. During your short time here, my dislike has grown. Everything you've said and done has given me annoyance. The sharpness of your tongue, your general manner of discontent. Your rejection of the friendly word . . .

RUTH. You lay it on a bit thick, don't you?

HENRY. Don't interrupt me. All these things I've seen, heard and disliked in you—then to my horror I found myself staring into a mirror. All these traits were my own, I had every fault I disliked in you—and with less excuse. I want you, at least, to understand, it isn't my environment that brought me failure here—I brought it myself—from within. I shall pray for us both, Mrs Stilton.

(RUTH *exits up* C.

The REVEREND MOTHER, BRIDGET *and* LUCY *enter* L. *They carry suitcases*)

REV. MOTHER (*looking at Lee*) Is he ill?
HENRY. He was exhausted. Mrs Stilton gave him a sedative.
REV. MOTHER (*putting down her case*) May God bless him, the poor man. (*She collects Schiller's case*) Mr Stilton has taken Father Schiller to the car at the side door, it will save him the verandah steps. Will you go, all of you?

BRIDGET, LUCY *and* HENRY *exit with their cases up* C. *The* REVEREND MOTHER *looks around for a few moments, crosses to the lamp* R, *turns it out, then collects her case and exits up* C.

MAGDALEN *enters slowly* L. *She goes to the window, peers out then moves* RC *and sees Lee. She stares at him for a moment then moves slowly to the armchair* LC. *She gazes at Lee once more, then from her habit she produces the General's letter. She removes it from the envelope and reads it slowly with tears running down her face. She then tears the letter in pieces and clenches the pieces in her hand. After a moment, she slowly opens her hand and the pieces of the letter drift to the floor. She sits in the armchair* LC *as*—

the CURTAIN *falls*

FURNITURE AND PROPERTY LIST

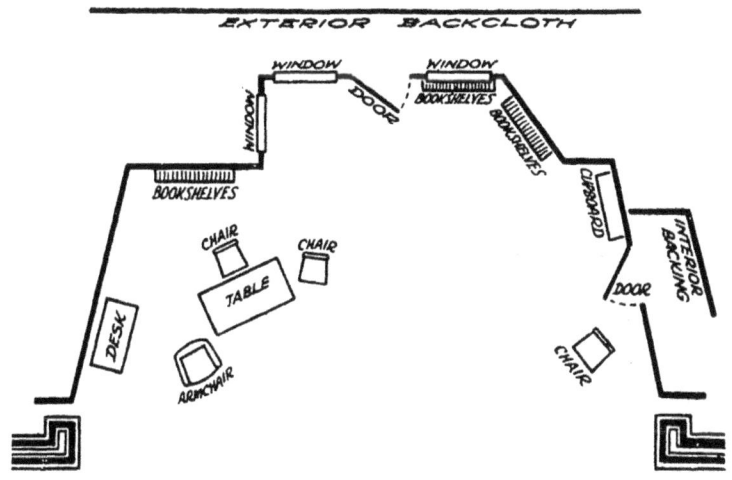

ACT I

On stage—Desk (R) *On it:* oil lamp
    On wall over desk: crucifix
    Table (RC). *On it:* books, stationary, inkstand, pen, pencils, list of books
    3 upright chairs
    Bamboo armchair
    Cupboard. *In it:* miscellaneous household articles, pliers, china salt cellar
    Bookshelves. *In them:* books
    On wall up L: bracket with oil lamp
Lamps out
Doors shut
Off stage—Sheet of paper (MAGDALEN)
    3 suitcases (STILTON)
    Tablet of soap (BRIDGET)
Personal—RUTH: handbag. *In it:* compact, case with cigarettes, matches
    STILTON: flask

ACT II

SCENE 1

Set—Large trunk (down LC)
    Pile of books (R of trunk)
Lamps lit
Doors shut
Off stage—Lighted cigarette (RUTH)
Personal—LEE: flask

Scene 2

Strike—Trunk
Set—*On armchair:* book
Lamps out
Doors shut
Off stage—2 suitcases (STILTON)
        Suitcase (RUTH)
Personal—STILTON: flask, letter
        LEE: flask

ACT III

Strike—Everything from shelves, desk and table
Set—*On table:* books and box for packing
Move armchair to LC
Doors closed
Lamp R, lit
Lamp L, out
Off stage—Black case. *In it:* hypodermic syringe, bottles of oil and drugs, swabs, prescription pad, pencil, kidney dish (HENRY)
        Suitcase (HENRY)
        Suitcase (REVEREND MOTHER)
        Suitcase (LUCY)
        Suitcase (BRIDGET)
        Letter (MAGDALEN)
Personal—HENRY: matches
        STILTON: cigarettes, matches

LIGHTING PLOT

Property Fittings Required—2 oil lamps
Interior. A Mission Common Room. The same scene throughout
THE APPARENT SOURCES OF LIGHT ARE—in daytime, windows up RC and up LC, and at night, oil lamps down R and up L
THE MAIN ACTING AREAS ARE—RC, LC and C

ACT I Afternoon

To open: Exterior—effect of bright sunshine
Interior—effect of shaded sunshine
Fittings off

No cues

ACT II SCENE 1 Evening

To open: Exterior—dark
Interior—effect of lamp light
Lamps lit

No cues

SCENE 2 Morning

To open: Lights as Act I
Fittings off

No cues

ACT III Evening

To open: Exterior—dark
Interior—effect of dim lamplight
Lamp R, lit

Cue 1 HENRY lights lamp L   (page 47)
Bring in lamp L
Bring up general lighting

Cue 2 The REVEREND MOTHER *turns out lamp* R   (page 60)
Take out lamp R
Reduce general lighting

EFFECTS PLOT

ACT I

Cue	1	LUCY: ". . . who it was?" *Sound of a car arriving and stopping*	(page 8)
Cue	2	REV. MOTHER: ". . . soon, Mrs Stilton." *Sound of a car starting up and driving away*	(page 15)

ACT II

SCENE 1

Cue	3	REV. MOTHER: ". . . the side door." *Shouts off* C	(page 31)

SCENE 2

No cues

ACT III

No cues

www.ingramcontent.com/pod-product-compliance
Ingram Content Group UK Ltd.
Pitfield, Milton Keynes, MK11 3LW, UK
UKHW021846210426
5322IPUK00022B/506